MESSAGES

Lynda Stephenson

ANNA MIRIAM PUBLISHING
12460 Crabapple Road, Suite 202 - 153
Alpharetta, Georgia 30201

Copyright 1997 by Lynda Stephenson
All rights reserved.
Printed in the United States of America.

ANNA MIRIAM PUBLISHING
12460 Crabapple Road, Suite   202 - 153
Alpharetta, Georgia 30201

ISBN 0-9656689-0-8
This book, cover, or parts thereof may not be reproduced in any form
without prior written permission of the publisher.

Unless otherwise noted, all Scripture quotations are from the
HOLY BIBLE, NEW INTERNATIONAL VERSION,
Copyright 1973, 1978, 1984,
by International Bible Society. Used by permission of
Zondervan Publishing House. All rights reserved.

Scripture Quotations marked GNB are taken from
The Good News Bible in Today's English Version, published by the
United Bible Societies. Old Testament: American Bible Society, 1976.
New Testament American Bible Society, 1966, 1971, 1976.

Cover Artwork
The Lion of Judah
By Lynda Stephenson

CONTENTS

INTRODUCTION 7

PART ONE
Healing Communications 10

PART TWO
In Search of the True God 50

*"...Do not weep! See, the Lion
of the tribe of Judah,
the Root of David,
has triumphed..."*

Revelations 5:5

*"Today, if you hear his voice
do not harden your hearts
as you did in the rebellion."*

Hebrews 2:15

*"Here I am! I stand at the door and knock..
If anyone hears my voice
and opens the door,
I will come in and eat with him,
and he with me.
To him who overcomes,
I will give the right to sit with me
on my throne, just as I overcame
and sat down with my Father
on his throne."*

Revelations 3:20, 21

INTRODUCTION

With an urgency increasing over time I have had a strong impression that I was to write a book. Yet any idea for a manuscript was remote, at best. The day came when I realized that my desire to write was given by God, but the words were not to be mine. They were to be His own words placed upon my heart.

In a time of preparation I began a process of healing and restoration. God led me to a ministry where His prophetic voice could counsel and encourage me. There, through an anointed prophet He gave me these words:

> Daughter, your life is about to take a whole new beginning. You find yourself in a time of transition. You feel a little confused. You feel ready to run on and do things, but you don't know even what the things are yet.
>
> I'm going to put you in a season of training unlike you've ever had before. I'm going to deposit things in you at a rate that you have never been able to receive them before.
>
> I'm going to wake you up in the night and I'm going to start to tell you things and you're going to write those things down lest you forget them. Because I'm going to speak to you personally.
>
> You desire a personal relationship. You are not satisfied with the relationship you have with Me right now. I'm not going to leave you there. I'm going to be faithful not to leave you there.

You've been pressing in and pressing in and wondering why you can't draw closer to My heart. This day the veil is rent. That veil, that wall that has had a cause, that has had an effect in you, that has prevented you from drawing close to Me is broken today. Your past is your past and you're walking a new life.

When you read things and you see things, sometimes you find yourself spooking, occasionally saying, "Can this really be of God? What am I sensing there?"

It's not spooky. It's real. I'm going to put a knowledge and an understanding of the Word inside of you unlike any that you've ever had in the past.

I'm going to give you a demonstration in the next month of something big in your life that is going to show you that I'm operating in a new way. You've been looking for something for the last six months, just something special with Me. When it comes, then something is going to rise up inside of you, and it's My Spirit. You're going to have the joy and you're going to have the power.

You feel that you lack power. You feel that you have the desire but you don't have the anointing. That's not so. The anointing is there, and now I'm going to begin to draw it out, and no one is going to stop it.

Now, press into Me for yourself. It's not a selfish thing to do. You've been one who's taken on everyone else's burdens. You've been a burden bearer even when it has not been Me who is asking you to take on those burdens. That is why you're tired. You're weary. You're exhausted and it's difficult to go on. You have even had a season where you felt like quitting. Someplace inside you felt like running and going on. Someplace inside you felt like quitting.

I'm going to teach you how to assume responsibilities that are Mine to take. You're not responsible for everything and you're not responsible for everybody. You're responsible only to be obedient to Me. I'm going to give you a clarity in your ears to hear My voice so that you won't be in confusion about should I do this or should I not do it. You're making yourself weary just trying to figure out what to do.

You're not going to miss Me. I am God, and I can speak loud enough and I can speak clearly enough that I can direct you and let you know what you need to do.

Soon I was to begin a journey of abundance. One week after I received this prophetic word, God kept His promise. Gently awaking at 3:30 in the morning I realized before I opened my eyes that I was mentally singing a familiar song. It was proclaiming God as The Mighty One of Israel. Even in songs and in dreams He was confirming His desire to speak to me and to His people.

Sleep-shrouded, I pulled up from bed, awakened my computer and began recording the first of many messages received night after night. These Messages are given here precisely as God spoke them into my heart.

Alpharetta, Georgia
March, 1996
L.S.

PART ONE

Healing Communications

Healing Communications

Yea, I Am God

Behold! He that keepeth Israel neither slumbers nor sleeps. I will not cause your foot to be moved. I will guide you with My hand, and by My righteousness you shall know Me. Yea, I am God.

You ask why I speak to you of Israel? It is because you have been wandering for forty years. Now I will lead you to your promised land flowing with milk and honey.

I am a faithful God. And I am mighty. You will know Me by My signs given to you. Watch for Me. Listen for Me. Pray to hear Me and My voice will fall upon you as the dew upon flowers, for you, too, are My beautiful flower. Trust Me to provide all your needs. I want you to know Me and Jesus, whom I sent. Now sleep, and trust Me to be faithful to My words.

I am He who watches and guards you. You are My precious sheep. I have many more yet out of the fold who need My care. I long to feed them the purest grass and give them cool, refreshing water.

You are to be one who helps Me find and gather My sheep. And I will not let you stray in the process.

Patience to Receive

I tell you, until you forsake all, you will not receive those blessings I have for you. You are to learn about multiplication of money in even small things before I trust you with great things.

But first, patience to receive. Abundant blessings will be yours. Trust me to fulfill all your desires. Go forward in faith, unafraid. Yield to Me as I lead you. I bless you, My child, My steward.

When I Take My Children Home

People say that I am not a loving God when I take My children home. Don't they know I let them come there of their own choosing, that they might grow spiritually?

In My spirit world it takes courage to become lower than the angels for a period of time. And it is My mercy that bids them home again. How foolish to think Me cruel by calling them again to say, "Well done. Come and rest here with Me. Your task on earth is over and you can return to your heavenly home."

Days Of Trials

So it is that you are led by the light of My Son, Jesus. And so it is that you follow Me to the glory of My Son. I am with you in days of trials. I am with you in the darkest night. By your faith you shall be known, and you shall lead others to My light.

Trust Me to care for you, to take care of you in every situation. Promise Me that you will follow wherever I lead.

Prepare, That I May Bless

Be of courage for I come to save you and My people, Israel. The heathen rage yet I hold out my hand to them all the day.

Go out in My vineyard. There you will find fruit ready for harvest. And I will show you which to harvest. They will be as kings among the laborers, so finely clothed are they.

And you, O prophet, will tell My word to them proclaiming My message of strength. For their strength perishes. They are not yet fit for labor. But I desire they be made fit and be clothed in righteousness.

And I say again, prepare! The vineyard is ready for harvest. I will make you ready to serve Me and My house. Honor Me in humility. Prepare the way that I may bless My seed.

You Will Hear

Behold, I stand at the door and knock. Do not be concerned. I will make My voice heard above the din of confusion.

You ask to be led. I will show you a more perfect way, and you will hear what I say. Trust Me.

Dominion

Yes, I called you even though this is not the hour you anticipated and no dream bids you to write. But I am with you as I promised. You are obedient and I will honor that.

Remember that I made man to have dominion over My

animals? You are not to fear horses. I will give you a calmness, a surety in your hand, in your step. And they, even they will know I sent you to help them.

In All Things, Order

So much I've promised you and you have waited patiently to see My revelations. Go now in peace to your tasks at hand and all will be opened to you. My hand is not shortened that it cannot save you from the destruction that had been planned.

You weary yourself in striving. Yet I promise the way to life in Me. Am I not the God who created you for good works? Will I stand afar and refuse your cries for help? Who am I that would refuse good things for My child?

Trust Me to bring all things in order — the good, and the evil to My submission. For I am a righteous and mighty God, capable of compassion and mercy.

And the gates of hell stand ready to receive your tormentors.

Be Not Dismayed

Why do you not heed My voice? I'm calling you to come into My house of submission and rest. I'm calling you to stand beside Me at the throne of grace and mercy.

Cleave not unto those whose wounds bind and hurt you. You must stand apart, alone if necessary, but apart with Me. I will be beside you in the trials. I will be there to comfort and befriend you. I will hold your hand as a father comforts and guides his child.

You truly are My child. I bid you come, and the way, My way is light. You shall not have to seek Me and My voice in silence much longer.

You are My sheep. I, the Good Shepherd. Trust Me to lead you, to care for you even as you care for these animals I have entrusted to you.

Rest. Be not dismayed over trials. I come to save.

I Will Supply

Let the redeemed of the Lord say so. And where are My people? Where are those who say, "I will serve my Lord?" They are standing behind bushes afraid they will be called.

It is not *their* words that deliver tidings of rescue and strength. It is not *their* strength and knowledge that will be called out from them. It is Mine, of Me, by Me, through Me.

I will use you if you are but willing. I will feed My flock from your hand.

Go now to the task I have set before you. It is My task, and I will supply the tools you need.

Bend in the Wind

These are the resting days. Soon I will open the road to a mighty work. You are preparing even now. You have sought Me. You have heard My call to you, "Come out." Be moved with My holy compassion and I will supply the strength and the opportunity for service.

Get your house in order for I will use it and you to supply rest for the weary. So much to do. So short a time. Bend in the wind as I lead you. Catch the fire of My Holy Spirit burning with a vengeance upon those who refuse My voice.

Show Me your heart ready for service and I will show you Mine, ever ready, ever hopeful that My will will convey hope and eternal rest within My house.

Lead to Me those who are blind. I long to heal their hearts and deliver them from worldly passions. This great gift of sight I give you for your use in spreading the joys of the wonders of My kingdom.

Rest now, preparing for the day of activation.

My Gates Will Open

Whatever may befall you I am there. Wherever the path leads I walk with you. You are My child. I am your Father. Come to know Me as a loving father loves his precious child. You do not understand this now, but trust Me to reveal Myself in the mysteries as they unfold. I will not keep you waiting on Me for answers to your heart's questions. I do love you.

All that you need Me to be I am. I am the Good Shepherd who guards and protects. I am the lover of your soul. I worry over you and send My angels to fight for you, to comfort you, to bring you to that place where no man can do you harm or injustice. Trust that they obey Me even as I trust you to obey Me. Carry out My wishes one by one as they are revealed to you. I will show you a more abundant life.

Keep hoping. Keep looking. My gates will open wide and you will see and you will know I have opened them for you. Enter now into a rest, that calm assurance of My hand leading, guiding you to your promised land. It is rich with the treasures of My love for you. Walk in the quiet ways. It is I who walk before you leading you to lighter days and a surer path.

Daniel 2:28 There is a God in heaven who reveals mysteries.

Child Of The Light

Yes, I am the Light. He who follows Me will not be lost in darkness. That is to say, he will be kept safe from evil.

You truly are a child of the light if you hear and obey My commands. And you say, "How hard it is to hear!" Then watch for Me to appear in familiar places. I walk among the lilies. I speak within the birds. In all things good I am found. If you look for Me, if you desire My presence you will seek and find Me.

I, too, desire your presence. I, too, seek you amid the storms and rainbows. It is I who call you to that place of My abiding, and will offer you a resting place within My arms.

No storm will assail you when I say, "Peace. Be still." You are to be found watching and waiting for My voice. Listen and you will hear.

I am mightier than the winds and more gentle than the grasses that are blown. Yet, I can make My presence known to those who truly seek Me.

Come with Me. The walk is cool and refreshing. I will speak with you and you will hear.

Rest From Your Worries

Yes, I am the Lord who speaks to you. In the quiet you hear My voice, small and quiet yet ever sure.

Don't worry about being weary, becoming tired. There is rest from your worries ahead. I am for you. You cannot reap a harvest without first plowing the fields and planting the seeds. It is I who plant. A few good seeds will take root.

I have planned the seasons carefully so that no storm or destruction removes My seed. They are growing in secret. But the harvest will be in the open — a joyful, abundant harvest! You will be there to enjoy the fruit of your labor, My love. Feast ye upon it!

I Am The Watchman

I am watching over you and your house. It is My home, too, and I jealously guard it. No thief will come in the night to take you away for you are My treasure. You may rest knowing I am the Watchman. You put your trust in My keeping power and I will protect you. Enter into restful sleep knowing I will guard you.

The battle for your soul is not over. But, fear not. You will be the victor as I walk before you shielding you from the forces that come to attack you.

I am more mighty than legions of your enemy. I will see to it that you prevail and justice is meted out to all. I am your Father who cherishes you.

Ease Their Suffering

I will provide a way for this healing of heart, mind and spirit. The day is coming soon when I will speak and those drawn close will hear and obey. You are to be used to soothe the suffering of My people.

Come to know My compassion, the desire of My heart to heal My lost children. I am waiting, waiting for one last detail to fall into place before sending you on that higher road of higher purpose. You will not go alone or empty, but you will be immersed in glory and filled with the strength of My hands. My body into yours to walk and lead the way to healing.

Where are My lost and crying? Strain to hear and answer as I speak through you to ease their suffering. You by My words will offer hope and promises to lift them into My presence. By your gifts they shall know Me as a righteous God, ever caring, ever watchful and loving, ever seeking them out from places of desperation.

Follow Me to your place of rest. There I will infuse you with the healing I have promised you. And many shall rejoice.

Tune Your Vision

Yes, I awakened you to hear My voice. You may believe Me when I tell you I desire your presence.

Swiftly falls the night around many left searching on their own without Me. Tune your vision that you may accurately see what I am willing to show you about My people.

They are lost, hungry for direction. Yet they know not the Way or the Hope. Because of their tiredness of heart I long to rescue. This, then, is their hope: to meet Me along the Emmaus road. And you will lead them.

What is My hope, My consolation without ones to share My work? You will go out in the highways and those will be ready to receive you. Have peace; have faith in My abiding. I am with you.

I Have Chosen The Path

I called. You came. And when I lead you will follow. Walk close behind in My footsteps. The path is one I have chosen for you and you shall be blessed. We go on an adventure where you will come to know Me, the great Father-God, the loving and caring companion.

Go swiftly for the night falls around you and I will keep you safe. Don't doubt that I come to protect and to lead you out of darkness to My Light. Hidden and secure you will rest. And peace surrounds your resting place, My place. You will rest, to soar again.

My Holy Gates

For surely, I call you. And if I call I will also lead you step by step. The way must not be so long. I long for you to bestow peace, My peace upon My people. Can you wait a little longer? Don't be impatient with the moving of My Spirit. It comes quickly. My righteousness will come upon you to be spread to these I send.

Where is My world? It is in darkness without the light of My Son. Show Me your willing heart. I will provide the means and way to a secure, abundant dwelling place within My walls. My walls, not those that have hindered. My walls of comfort and protection. My walls, entered by My gates now opening wide to receive many.

Help Me provide this security to My lost and helpless ones. I come that they might have life and have it abundantly. The course is straight that leads to My holy gates. Enter in and be blessed for I am with you.

The sheep gate, the sheep gate! Follow Me and I will care for you, My precious sheep.

A Life of Freedom

I am your Father who cares for you. My message is the same: Be thou perfect even as Jesus is perfect.

And you ask, "How?"

Your daily communion with Me is the answer, for I am the Light, given to you to make your weary path a ground for rejoicing. I make your trials as light as day, as easy as night following the day.

My wish for you is a life of freedom and you are walking in it now. My hand is upon you, blessing you, showing you the way. It is no accident that you have come the long way home for I needed you to recognize My saving power, My grace.

By your experience you are equipped for the job ahead for many people await release from bondage that you, too, have known. By My grace and wisdom you shall set them free to go in peace.

Where I send you I first prepare the way. The way is being made ready to receive Me. I am calling you out in the highway. So hear My voice as you go. I am with you, speaking. Though soft, you will hear. Answer Me in your heart and I will show you what to do that My name be praised and My people set free. Go in peace.

A Willing Heart

There is so much to tell you, to lay upon your heart. Hear thou My people lost and crying in their self-made wilderness. I have a plan for their redemption and a plan to lead you to their doorstep. The door will be unlatched for you to enter in and bring My message, My saving grace with you.

It is still yet dark before that great dawn. You still have much to do, much to learn before I send you out. I shall put a heart within you that is willing and able to love them as I love you. Ever kind, ever present in spirit, you will be ever ready to give and receive My commands.

Go with thanksgiving. I will open the path before you and I will bless and heal these through your hand. Do not neglect My tasks however small, yours to complete in My mercy.

Honor Me

My child, whether or not you hear Me depends on your obedience. I will call you with a trumpet, a loud voice. You will hear and know that I have spoken and even that I open your ears to hear.

Praise in the sanctuary results in praise at the throne. Begin there and I will give new songs words for you to sing. Above all, honor Me with the gifts I give you and all supply for them and their use will come.

Covet My Word!

Peace Amid the Storm

For whosoever shall call upon the name of the Lord shall be saved and his house. Yes, you sanctify your loved ones by your faith in Me and My saving ability. Let the redeemed of the Lord say so.

Say to all who enter, "The Lord is my God and Him only shall I serve." Your works, your life ever progressing, ever pressing toward the goal, My goal, will be a witness to these around you. And by your faith many shall be set free.

Hold fast to that which is good. Cling to My goodness found each day even in trials and tribulations patiently borne.

Those who have eyes to see, let them see. I will impress upon the heart of those who love Me an image of the beauty of My creation, even that peace found amid the storm. For I will call him beautiful who waits upon Me.

Surely, the Lord is in this house. My children are to *be* the peace found amid the storm.

Worrisome Father

These are the souls who long for Me. These are the days that find them waiting on My word. These are the lost, the lonely without My companionship to comfort them.

You ask, "Who, Lord? Who are these You speak of?" And I tell you they are all around you. They hunger and are not filled. Their thirst is not quenched.

Yet, I long and wait. I seek them to fulfill their deepest or smallest need. I am a worrisome father who broods over His children.

Be thou sufficient to show the way to Me and My house. A big command? Yes. But it is I who wait on you to go and do and serve. Enter into My courts and see the great blessings in store for you and for those you lead to Me.

Floodgates of Manna

Whatever I say or tell you is real and can be believed. I am for you. I am watching and guiding your step. Enter now into a peaceful glade as I go to war for you clearing away the stones in your path. You shall enter My gates with thanksgiving, and they will see My glory who wait upon Me.

I, your Lord prepare a brighter day for you and I long to give of My blessings to you and My people. They are coming home and you are to be My helper. Show them the way to a glad reunion.

Thou art My child. I know your needs and prepare for them. Why doubt My goodness in all things? Abundant supply of all you need is promised. Floodgates of manna will open to you and you will be filled. Yes, you and your house.

Go in peace and I will supply your need before you are even aware it exists. Follow thou Me.

The Way to Contentment

Enter, enter in and wait and I will answer in the most wonderful way, a way yet to be discovered by you. No, you need not die before receiving these blessings, this freedom.

Only die to self, selfish desires. I will show you the way to peace and contentment. But first, trust Me to handle all your cares. Put them before Me and wait. As hard as that seems it is timely. Come into My presence with praise. I go before you.

This Christmastide

You seek Me, yet I also seek you. Amid the debris of days and nights of anguish your voice is heard.

So hear Me. I come, the Babe, the still, small voice, the cry to all mankind, "Come to the manger and receive new life, new hope in an unclean world."That is their salvation, their freedom from servanthood to masters of self that lead only to confusion, destruction.

Oh, lonely world! Find in Me the loving arms of a father who longs to comfort, to offer peace if you but come to Me, the Father, the Babe. Hear Bethlehem's eternal message: Come thou and be blessed with peace and with forgiveness of all that restrains your peace. Receive My gift this Christmastide: hope for newness of life, and the peace that follows hope.

Water My Garden

You are tired, but soon I bring you to life. For verily, I am calling you, have called your name, and My voice shall be true. You shall lead many to Me, and these you love I love with a holy vengeance.

Water My garden. I have planted seeds of righteousness. With your kindness, with mercy, with truth of My divinity water My garden. By doing so coals are heaped upon them setting a fire within them to know what goodness is Mine.

Enter now with faith that you shall see fruit, a wellspring of My labor in you. Comfort ye My people. Those you love will come to Me in My time. A mighty and sovereign God am I, able to justify, that is, to proclaim blameless, the world awaiting salvation. My peace awaits you and those I call.

Out Of The Old Year

Enter into new hope, a new path planned and decided by Me, your Savior. Come before Me in thanks that all will be well with those whose Lord I am.

I Am, that they should seek and find Me. I Am, that they may hope and joy in My presence. I Am to those lonely and lost without Me, I Am the Light.

Hungry? Be fed of Me and live. Thirsty? By righteousness be quenched and filled. Hold your cup beneath My fountain and be filled to overflowing.

Out of despondency of the old year, its pain and deeds of death, these leave behind, rags no more needed. Clean and white are the clothes I give you, new hope to be worn in My design for living a purer life.

Walk with Me in newness of life. I offer hope, rest to the weary, and the peace that abides in this, your loving Father's home.

Expect Joy

Blessed are the peacemakers for they shall be called the children of God. And have I not called you My child?

Weep not that men have not found the way in Me, but expect to see joy on their faces as they come to recognize the One True God. And you shall lead them. Yes, even you, for by My stripes you are healed and by My sorrows you have been made worthy to bring others unto Me.

It is no mystical thing when others see My face and go away rejoicing, but it is a mystery as to how I work to bring them to that place. You are but My emissary, a child of My womb and yes, a peacemaker. Is this too powerful to receive? No, not in My time, My circumstance. Remember that it is My time, chosen to bless these I call and these I send to you.

You will be found worthy.

Oh, The Wonder!

My light that I have placed within you to shine for many will open a pathway of hope and inspiration. And a little child shall lead them — My child.

Go in faith that words will guide and bless you and those for whom My Word means life. Oh, the wonder! The wonder of My love for you. Enter now into that peaceful, expectant place of service. I walk before you shielding the way and guiding your step.

Ezekiel 36:27 And I will put My Spirit within you and cause you to walk in My statutes, and you shall keep My ordinances and do them.

Wind Of Change

Yes, the time is near when I call and you obey, hearing My voice. You shall be taught and led. I shall hold open the door to My inner sanctuary where you shall be refreshed with My anointings for you.

Out of that place, that intimate place of My abiding shall come a newness of life for you and for those whose lives you touch. I am to be a living force to be reckoned with, a mighty wind of change within many. You shall see and know it is I and by My hand that healing flows.

Oh, give thanks at My holy gates. Pray that they open wide to receive My called, and pray to lead the way to My mercy and forgiveness. You are soon coming to that place of rest where you hear and know My call upon you. Watch in the days ahead for My sign, My gift to you of My love and My call upon you.

You desire to be blessed and to bless others. I will come and I will be faithful to keep that sacred which has been committed to Me. You are My child and I love you.

Press in, for I am guiding you to a surety in Me.

Give Me Your Cares

Say unto Me, "These things are in Your hands and I trust You to reveal them." Then leave them with Me. I do care about your concerns, these fears based on your past experience. I do care and desire freedom for you.

Do you not think Me capable of attending to your needs? Am I without compassion for My children?

Under My Wings

The Lord thy God shall cover thee with His wings. None shall assail you in My care. I am God and under the shadow of My wings you may soar or glide without fear.

I am mighty. Before Me and behind Me there is no other force that can match My covering. Trust Me to hold you up, to gird you with truth, to cradle you in majestic yet tender arms, My arms of love for you.

I am proud of you and your progress. Learn to trust Me even more and I will send you afar, unknowing, yet ever sure of My presence and My command upon your life.

With Me you shall be the conqueror, the healer, the light to many. You must trust Me for in the days ahead your feet will cross stormy waters before reaching that place of peace. It must be for your victory over Satan to be won. Together we will conquer your foes and the foes of many. Trust Me to lead you to a higher plain of service and a deeper knowledge of My source, My power to overcome with majesty and mercy.

Don't be afraid. The victory is yours. By My hand you shall be healed. First, the healing, and then the healed. I am able to keep you from falling. Hold on. I come swiftly to rescue you and put your feet on solid ground. I am your God who loves you. Learn of Me how great I am and how great is My love for you.

Faith Gathering

I, the Lord, speak to you in the grandest way, solemn and sure, and yet you doubt Me still. So you do not see majestic acts. They will come to those that you may see and be blessed.

Enter now into a time of faith gathering to gird and prepare you for your mission ahead. No, not one of Mine shall be lost. Be content to wait as I open doors for the lost and needy.

A Beautiful Plan

You are angry with Me for I do not speak as you demand nor do I obey you. Do you choose to forget the changes wrought in your life?

Am I not moving fast enough? Do My words fall on deaf ears or are you missing Me completely? You are not listening nor believing when I say you will be moved to higher ground, you will be sent to those lost and wandering without Me.

Yet, still, you want answers in your way, in your time. Have I been so strong a God not to feel remorse over you that My anger at your avengers ceases? I am not remorseful over you, that is, guilty, for I am not complacent. Indeed, I am actively angry with your enemies.

No. In My time, My time I answer. It is a perfection I am working in you. Don't be an insolent child who behaves with a stubborn will refusing My voice to you.

See Me, still. Return day upon day, night upon night to My presence. Here you will find Me waiting to do your bidding. But come in love and faith in My abiding wisdom. You cannot see all that I am moving out of your path that you stumble no more. Give Me praise and thanksgiving. Ask for more faith to see you through to the next step. So it shall be done unto you as you do to others.

Be thankful for our time together, this time of quiet deliberation, of just communion. I am your Father who loves you, but a rebellious child is untrainable. I understand your impatience to see great works, to hear Me in the workplace, to have that affirmation upon your life of My care and guidance.

Call Me Blessed Hope. I am the Rock upon which to build this new life. I build block by block according to My design and plan. Trust that it is a beautiful plan for your life.

The Wheels Are In Motion

You shall rise up and call Me Blessed. The wheels are in motion for the coming of the Lord. And you shall see in triumph My majesty before you.

My called are being readied. Yes, you, even you will call My name Wonderful, as in a shout! You, too, will rise in the air to meet Me.

What glory! The transfiguration of My called. You are to be among those I desire with Me on that great and horrible day. Like lambs to the slaughter we will go. But before that, the blessed peace I impart to My church.

Keep watching, ever waiting for My Word, My Glory, and be not consumed on that holy day. I am He who promised a mighty sword and victory to My overcomers. Rise with Me even this day for the hour of your transfiguration is near. I have said, "Prepare the way and you will be blessed among My people, all ye who serve Me and know My name."

Oh, sing unto Me, and I will shower new songs of praise upon your lips.

Grow In Grace

Now is the time to get ready. Do you want a song? Do you want something new in your life? How grows the down on a duck's back? It is ever sure, but growing close without notice even to the duck.

So you, too, are growing in grace. Tiny feathers to protect you, to keep you warm, to insulate your body as it were, are growing in spite of your inability to see them.

I have made you and am making you ready for the swim ahead. It will be as natural as a duck swimming in the water, and how you love the water! My refreshing, My comfort, My freedom are yours to float in My care completely at ease. A natural grace I give you — no, that you've not yet seen. It is there, upgirded by My love as the water upgirds My ducks.

Thank you for loving my nature. It blesses you as I meant it to. I can use it through you, your love, to bless other people. Come follow Me. You will see and enjoy My beauty with new eyes and a new heart worthy of this passion for My creation that I have placed within you. You don't understand? But you will. Thank Me. Rejoice even more of My hand working in this world painting great designs upon My palette.

I give you grace to paint, too. You are unsuspecting of gifts yet to flow. You will show My love through your work and shout the victory as others see Me in your work and come with gladness before Me.

Look forward to a new work. It is coming soon. I am opening a way to bless and use you.

Await The Touch

What is thine to give is of Me, My life-bread manna for many who seek and do not know it is Me they seek.

What is yours to give? Yes, a touch, but it is more than that. It is your faith that others may see and rejoice, that hope be born anew in mind and heart and that praise emanate from holy grounds — simple, but holy grounds.

You do My bidding by going to work touching these whom I send. Not whom you call are they but whom I send. Don't forget, it is My work to bring them to that place of hearing, that place of delighting in Me. No more will they reject the Father who loves them, the Son who died that they might live, the breath of the Holy Spirit moving, ever moving, stirring a love to win them to Myself.

Come before Me. Kneel, bow, be still and await the touch of My presence, My countenance upon you. You will glorify My name. I have spoken it. Rejoice!

Peaceful Day Coming

I, the Lord, am one God. I know your heart and I know your body, mind and spirit. Then I know the needs in every area of your being. Bring them to Me for healing, for restoration.

My desire is to walk with you, healing, blessing, being a thoughtful companion, being someone, yes, someone who hears and understands your deepest thought and care. Remember the Last Supper with My disciples? I washed their feet, I fed them, I ministered to them even though it was I who was about to embark on a dark and painful journey.

Yes, I was teaching them. But, I, too, needed their companionship even in the dark hour. I needed to know they loved Me for who I was, not for what I could do in miracles and works.

So you, too, need to know I enjoy your companionship. Even as you seek Me, seek to hear My words unto you, I am waiting to open doors of wisdom and understanding of My travails to you. You must know My pain as I know yours. Is this not the sharing of true companions?

Together we shall feed My flocks with the mercy of human kindness which is My Father's gift. Mercy, unfolding, flowing over, bathed in the light of My love for you.

If you don't understand My love for you, then understand the love of the Father for His child. All will be provided that that one might prosper, grow in grace and maturity with a firm conviction of his purpose in this life.

You, too, will know the purpose for which you are designed to fulfill by My mercy and in My name. The Light ever seeks to shine on you, before you.

Call Me Blessed Comforter of My children. I show a more glorious way to My righteousness. There is salve for your wounds and a new and peaceful day coming ahead.

Trust Me to deliver you from your persecutors, to bind your wounds washed with My tears for you.

New Wine

I am the Vine; ye are the branches. From the Vine the sweetest wine flows, the wine of My Spirit. It is a new refreshing I long to give you. Drink of Me, My Word. Follow in My footsteps to the Tree of Life, My life ever opening before you.

The new wine of My gospels awaits many ready to receive My life-giving blood. It is of Me they hope. It is My body that makes them whole. Bring them to Me for My ministrations and I will give them the wine of new life. It is a joy, a fulfilling of the prophecies which awaits you.

Journey Of Adventure

This, even this shall come to pass: they shall be stretched and sewn, to be stretched again in more patterns awaiting discovery.

As fabric is stretched over the wings smoothly without tears to made a flyable instrument, so will your wings be stretched and sewn. My Father's design is unique, established just for you. This partnership newly entered, will be for My purpose, and so you will know My will is in the design.

Call My name Wonderful Host of Heaven. I will open a new doorway for you to fly to My works, My plans. You are just beginning a journey of adventure.

Be brave. Be bold! It is My hand upholding and guiding your vision. Trust Me to lead you safely, securely.

Use Your Days Wisely

I, even I have spoken to you concerning this vision of wholeness where nations rise up to meet Me and I receive them. Yet, departing are they now into a moral abyss so far from My righteousness are they.

You must be concerned. You must be trained for I will raise you up to tread the path for My people. The dust that gathers in your skirt shall be shaken out, washed clean. As these are humbled, bowed before Me in humility My glory will flow as peace comes to wash over and through the land of My calling.

Yes, go now to your work of preparation. I give you guidance and strength. Those will come to show the way, My path of service laid before you. Take My hand. Take My name to these I place in your path. They will receive My blessings and you will know I have sent you. Follow closely. The pleasure of days in My presence is coming soon.

You must plan. You must plan. You must plan and use your days wisely. I will provide strength to your body, food for your soul. But you must plan. Do not let idleness overtake the time of preparation I give you. Use it thoroughly for My time to use you is coming as night closes before the day.

Day Of Reckoning

I, the Lord, have told you to watch and wait on My day of reckoning. If pride goeth before a fall then pride it is that makes you to stumble. The pit is always ready, gaping wide to receive pride's victims.

You say this seems harsh to you? Such lessons come harshly. You who are Mine receive My voice and obey. Those who turn against Me, My call, cry from the pit for My rescue.

I am a God of humble pity. I turn to them again, lifting their hopes to newer levels, washing their concerns as a mother bathes her child. It is I who watch with care over My lost child. I stand ready to hear My name called so that I may run and scoop them up into My arms.

Yes, a mother, too, I am to My children. But I am the same God you know as your Father. There is no confusion in My house over who calls My name holy.

Be true to My commands to reach these in search of the True God. I am He, yes, He who made you to walk in likeness of Me. Go ahead. Write! I write with you that all know the truth.

What babe cries for his mother and she refuses his cry? Not I, his mother, father, sister, brother, friend. I hear. I answer. I come to rescue, to comfort, to give needed suckle with the milk of human kindness.

You are like sheep gone astray, wandering from My fold. Enter in in blind faith that in the dark night I care for you. My sheep hear My voice and do not question their master's leading. So, too, I call, I lead, I comfort and care for you. Enter in and be filled. My flock awaits reconciliation with the Master Shepherd. They search in vain who seek another's voice.

I am sufficient. I am sufficient for all your needs. No other cares for you as I do. I am He who made you, questioning, searching. *I am sufficient.*

Zion Calls

I am the Lord, and I remove even those circumstances that hinder you and your work. It is coming, that day for gathering in My people. My covenant is with them beyond their understanding.

Have you not said, "Thy will be done"? My will is to use you. Behold the doorway into My presence. Leave behind your earthly cares, for they fall away in the face of My mighty acts. You, too, will enter the sheep gate as one of My covenant.

Walk tirelessly now. I give you strength and wings to uphold you. The light is dawning upon a new day when the weary shall run and not faint, and many by My leading will come in and wait before Me.

Weep, for the night is pressing in. Mourn for many who reject My call. The song of Zion calls, a faint echo of the past. It sings still to all who would but hear.

My Angels

Little steps, little faith become mighty in patient testing. Winged serpents meet their foe, My angels in battle over you. Praise Me for their victory.

It is a mighty battle. Don't forget them, their mission to fulfill on your behalf.

Prepare By Singing

Listen when I say I have a purpose for you. You will see it soon for surely My hand is moving to prepare you. You are right when you say the night is not yet over.

Hear the birds singing as daybreak beckons them to a new day. How sweet the sounds of their music filling the dark sky. They sense what you cannot see, the rising of the sun. They prepare by singing and waiting for the light. They are assured it is coming.

Lay down your burdens one more time. Dispel the gloom with a singing heart. Ideas I give you. People I bring you to share your heart's desire. A full life, yes, in abundance is My desire for you, and your desire to be used is My delight.

Can you see it is My hope I've placed within you to serve? Shower Me in this time with praise, for this is the music that wakens My ears to your bidding.

Holy is the host of angels singing before Me who see the triumph planned for you.

Perfect Timing

You must see the need now that preparation is necessary. I will not cause you to get out before people empty of word or thought unable to do My bidding.

I am a tireless God who instructs, plans, and waits for perfect timing for My instruments to sound in harmony according to precise instruction. You will hear My cue. My call will not find you rushing, rushing without complete readiness, and you will arrive on time.

Allow Me to prepare the script, the music, and the timing suitable for action, for performance. Don't fear that since My music is already playing that there is not an interval for your precise entry.

I love you and I hear your voice. It's not too late for you to join My mighty chorus. Continue in prayer and preparation. Your song will be heard, although silent now. But wait. I come to lead you.

In Facing Surgery

Yes, I am on your side. You can be sure of My command to go forth in freedom. I, your servant, will command forces of healing to wrap you, cover you, protect your body in the healing process. You will walk with newness of life. I speak a peace to you concerning this.

I am the Great Physician, healing, binding wounds, creating newness in features that hold you captive. Your task is to be healed. I will provide the way, for surely your pain shall be erased.

Go in peace. I go before you preparing those to serve you. You shall be free for I work all things for your good and for your good nature to be used to bless others.

When You Feel Vulnerable

When you feel vulnerable, speak only in the spirit for other spirits cannot discern this voice. You need go no further than to utter My name.

Show Me only the pureness of your desire to win souls for Me. I will take care of the rest. Your awakening I allow. I guard your thoughts from those not of Me.

Safely I lead you into unknown worlds of conflicting thought. You wander where I have sent angels on either side of you. Claim their presence.

Remember, it is My battle, it is My victory. Forces beyond your understanding tremble in anger and fear at My name. I hear your cry to run from this battle. Run, you must, leaving it in My hands. I deliver you from darkness. War over that darkness, but leave the victory to Me. I come to rescue you, My warrior. You are stepping into the unknown. But the unknown is My territory. I am with you. My rod and My staff lead you, comfort your steps. You desire not to stray. I will keep you, your path safe. An awakening to things of God is coming. You cannot bear what you cannot see in battle. But trust Me to lead you.

Am I not the conqueror? Leave all to Me. I have sent you because I am a mighty warrior, not because you are mighty.

Music Of The Spheres

I promised to take care of these pains and disillusions. I promised to carry you over the waters of adversity and to gently set your feet on solid ground.

Where I promise, I make the way clear to receive it. So even now, cast your burdens upon Me. Enter in. Prayer, praise, thanksgiving provide a path for My answer.

Your heart breaks with its cares. Even as I hear you I work wonders of mercy for your reconciliation. Keep high your hands to receive My blessings. You will receive what I plan for your awakening in spirit and adventure.

Thank Me that all things shall be made new, even that victory awaiting release from poverty of spirit. I will rejoice with you. My band of angels dance with the music of the spheres in anticipation of My glory to be shown.

Praise Me, praise Me, praise Me! Abundant offerings of praise become abundant offerings of love turned to meet your needs as only I can do.

Don't be downcast or sorrowful. A new day of glory will shine through this veil and you are to be richly blessed for your perseverance. If you but hope in Me I will bring light to your doorstep and peace to nations.

So shall you rise up that others may hear and know I am God.

The Earth Groans

I am a mighty God whose wrath covers the earth. They who dwell therein are to see My wrath with a vengeance if they do not listen.

How the earth groans with her travail! How it shudders with the density of her pain! You do not hear the cry of her labor to force you to action, to ask for change in your habits.

You are most guilty who love her for the sun rises and sets daily upon her destruction. Believe Me when I tell you her time is short. Believe the sounds coming forth as trumpets blaring a new dawn. Close your ears no more and warn those living in the wasteland: "Hear the word of the Lord! His day of triumph is coming like a thief in the night which catches the unprepared. Get ready to move your belongings and your household to higher ground."

The seas shall cover a mighty land before the Day of the Lord is revealed. Run, though weary, to dry and arid regions. Leave behind your glory amid the suffering of humanity. Call forth, "When the Lord prepares the way I will go." Follow Me to the foothills. Rejoice with Me that the end is seen in the beginning of these signs.

God has spoken to prosper His people amid the grief of towns covered in their disbelief. Whole cities fall victim to their own decay. The Alpha and the Omega I am. All things shall be brought low because of My anger.

My pity is saved for those who hear the cries and obey. Be faithful and I will be faithful to bring you through. Cast your fear upon Me and pray. Pray for My sovereign mercy and quick judgement.

The day comes quickly. Gather in your sheep. An army comes to destroy them, but My hand leads you into safety. Hear thou My words to you concerning this. I am mighty to save, swift to hear. Call My name before you and that day shall be shortened that renders you helpless against your foe.

Now, watch and wait.

Warn My People

No man will listen except you go to tell him. None understand except you convey the message of deliverance.

It is a divine calling I give you and you must act. Yes, write the book. I am giving you even now the tools, the knowledge, the inspiration. Write as I instruct, word by word, page by page as I give it unto you.

The die is cast, as it is said. Warn My people, Israel, to build on high places. They, too, need to know I come for them.

Prepare this day a manuscript of heavenly proportions to be given them in book form. No, you can't of your own accord accomplish this work, but I, working through you can move mountains of insecurity and give places of refuge to My people.

Write! All will be as I have proclaimed. By My hand you shall reach many.

Isaiah 44:26 and 27 GNB: But when my servant makes a prediction, when I send a messenger to reveal my plans, I made those plans and predictions come true. I tell Jerusalem that people will live there again and the cities of Judah that they will be rebuilt. Those cities will rise from the ruins. With a word of command I dry up the ocean.

Matthew 24:15, 16: So when you see standing in the holy place 'the abomination that causes desolation' spoken of through the prophet Daniel — let the reader understand — then let those who are in Judea flee to the mountains.

Love More Fully

It is My desire to heal, not just your desire that that one be washed, healed and set free from all doubts and disillusions. It is My will to take him into My house, My chambers and speak with him anointing him with the oil of mercy, forgiveness and truth.

I call him now. I call him. Obey Me when I tell you I come to walk there with you binding sorrows of the past and asking your forgiveness upon him. He needs your forgiveness as I need you to forgive.

I will provide the way, the healing, the mercy that leads you to freedom in this. Oh, it is hard, that meting out of mercy from pain. Yet, seek to do this and all will fall down around you. Walls of fear, walls of secrecy fall in the face of My mercy, yours to bestow. Surely you will be filled with loving kindness, and the power to overcome your foe is found in this love.

I Am Truth

Holy, Holy is My name above all the others, above any who seek to be revealed through other channels, other means. Let this be a sign: My name proclaimed in places far beyond the bounds of human consciousness. Because you seek truth above all designs of human frailty, I am Truth and lead you into Me.

My righteousness prevails. Don't forget that. Don't follow darkness' path to disillusion. You shall know My name as Holy, Protector, Keeper of Wisdom and Justice.

Bow Down And Wait

Bow down before Me. Wait there for I desire to tell you many things in secret which will later be opened to others. It is ready, this coming of ages past to hear My voice and My call. Enter before Me in praise, awaiting My voice. How lovely beyond all human knowledge is My Word, My Word described in thought, My sovereign yet simple Word.

I desire to be fully yet easily understood as supreme and loving. In the realm of consciousness and beyond it is My Word that calls you to come before My heart panting with desire for you. Within the bounds of present wisdom I seem distant, a future odyssey to behold and to perform sanctimonious deeds.

YEA, I AM MORE.

On Higher Plains

I am a merciful God who desires your unending faith through trials and troubles. Yet, I cling to your longings for mercy and abate them swiftly. Hear My cry to overcome your enemies of disillusion, discouragement, and hopelessness for things of the future.

Your battle must be won on higher plains than you can see, and I fight them for you in courts of My design.

My Land Trembles

My land trembles and quakes. Yea, hear ye and obey. I am making a way in the desert for those willing to hear Me as I call them out of the lands now coming forth to bend and shake them from their apathy.

You will be led. You will be sent to warn the few waiting for My Word. I will open the way, supply the money, send the faithful to gather Mine.

Do you have the courage? Oh, pray for boldness to announce My coming glory upon the land. Be smitten with jealous fury over those who are lost and seeking salvation.

You are My light reflecting My Son. A sovereign will is Mine to cherish and protect you along the way. Enter into more praise daily. Pray for guidance and the sure sign of My leading.

Angels Await

My desire is to bring in those truth-seekers who are following the dictates of false prophets. Some will come who least believe now. Precious is the gift of friends who lead forward to the gateway of truth.

You will see it soon and coming at My hand. My angels await to serve, to guide, opening doors before you that the way be prepared before your entry. Heal, heal, heal the broken-hearted, the lame and yes, the blind. My wounds cover many sins and many await healing ministrations.

Do not fret. The glory will be Mine as is the power to make believers out of these to whom you speak healing words of wisdom. My love and My light go with you.

Submit Changes To Me

Submit to me the changes you desire and that I desire for you. I will take them, cleanse and mold a more purified conception of your being.

Trust Me to bring you through, even to initiate and to complete this process. It is necessary.

You Are My Voice

Oh, Jerusalem! My city caught in despair of its travails. Oh, earth! Mourn that My task be quickly fulfilled, that you be healed from destruction that comes swiftly now.

Oh, Jerusalem! Ye are My chosen to lead many to Me out of darkness. Darkness comes, and is even there, but it will be scattered upon the earth whose destruction comes nigh.

Hallow My name; keep it ever before you. There are those who call and proclaim God as holy who seek the righteousness of divine will, the preservation of their mortal souls. My plan is destruction to unrighteousness. My bidding deems necessary the destruction of evil calling itself good and holy.

Oh, mourn and weep that destruction be swift, that you who seek My divine will be lifted quickly from its snare, that righteousness prevail around you and your dominion.

Help those in need of My care to hear My voice, My voice, My voice! You are My voice to many. Enter My presence with praise and thanksgiving that you will be shown the way to lead those into My glory. Be ever thankful that your day is soon coming when others may know My name. And you will be used to tell it to them.

Planner Of Dreams

My child, listen when I say to you that I call you to a wider place in the road. This place shall flow with the dreams of many people. It will be open to their visions, visions that I give them. You will invite them to share this place of your dreams with you.

I can use you. I can use your dream to fulfill My hopes for many in that place of My abiding. Do not worry about being distant from relatives, family, friends. I will bring them to you and you won't be lonely or afraid. I go ahead to prepare the place, the people to receive you and the money you will have to offer.

What a wonderful blessing I plan. I see it now beginning to form on a bright and new horizon of My making. Include Me in these hopes. See Me as planner of your dreams, giver of them to you. I have many great treasures awaiting your discovery.

Get ready. Sit at your planning table. As I said before, plan, plan, plan. It is this that I told you to plan for. It is possible that a new beginning of many good and precious things is in store for you.

I love you and want to share rich blessings with you. My people shall be the people who come to enjoy this habitat with you.

Rest. Hope. Anticipate that a new and glorious day is coming and is yet on the horizon.

PART TWO

In Search of the True God

In Search of the True God

This Is The Blessing

This is the book I have ordained. This is the blessing I long to give that many will see Me within its pages and believing, may find wholeness, a healing draught drawn therein.

You must hear Me now. I can't wait longer for your timing. It is time. Begin however you can. I stand with pen in hand moving to bless your page with echoes of My desires for mankind. Hurry to the task. I will guide you each step of the way.

I'll provide the manuscript. Take steps to ensure the progress of it. Your tools must be at the ready for I delay no longer. Delight in this project, an answer to your prayers as well as a salve for nations awaiting My healing communications.

The Book

Count among your blessings the gift to convey by writing My message of hope. Sit down in faith to write. Be faithful. Daily set your vision on My calling to witness to My call to you.

Be ever faithful. I am He who calls. I will prosper the words given unto you to reap a harvest of Mine own waiting to hear. But you must write as I tell you. You obey Me. I will bless your work and others shall see Me in it. It is a mighty act, a mighty word to be given.

Pray for divine instruction. My name awaits the praises of those who long to hear the voice of My prophets. And so you shall deliver sons and daughters by your hand. Yes, I am He who calls you to this purpose. Go boldly, now. Prepare the manuscript of My Father's work in the heavens that that day be rejoiced over many.

Pray For Truth

The Lord thy God leads. Out of barrenness of spirit the womb cries for fullness, that hope be born. That Hope is the Lord God for whom you search. In vain do you look to the mountains for your God is to be found among His people and in their hearts.

That loneliness you feel, that fear that circles you like some mad dog is but your doubt and unknowing of truth. Pray for truth. Pray to recognize truth when she comes.

Hear what the Lord God says to you concerning the prophets. They are among you, scattered about yet joined in purpose: to bring My word of My coming kingdom to you.

Forgiveness

Daily lay down idols of your past. Seek to recognize them and call them by name as you cast them at My feet. I bind them in your presence as you call them out.

Persevere, never looking back upon those things that the enemy would bring to your memory, those things that I have forgiven. In faith - faith, not feelings, forgive the wrongs done unto you.

Forgiveness is the next act of cleansing and perfecting. I will see you through this painful veil. This time your tears will prove worthy.

You Have Been Blessed

Follow your heart's desire in the marketplace. I am beginning to open to those around you a message of your impending success. It depends, this success, on timing that is like no other has been nor will be again. A stroke of good will intends to sear your heart. You will shout for joy and call your neighbors and friends to celebrate with you. From their hearts as thick and dry as hardened leather they will feel hope spring anew. It is but a measure of My love for you that will give them questions concerning Me.

Do you have the answers? Do you yet know what I bring in the way of hope or revelation? Your nation has rejected the words of My prophets, seeming only to look for what has already been sent.

You have been blessed by the Almighty with wisdom, if you but leave the discerning of it to Me. Instead, there has been little grace with which to measure this wisdom. It has become a god in itself, holding court to judge the hearts and deeds of others.

This is not what your blessing was intended to be. How can blessings in one proceed to be a curse, your judgement upon another?

Hope In My Presence

My majesty is shown to any who would hope in My presence, pray for revelation of My working here. It is not in vain that I have waited desiring you to come into the fold of My own. Those desiring Me shall be released to new life as I have promised: new life, abundant, flowing down, washing over and pardoning transgressions. This cleansing is but a part of this new life, this new beginning to prepare you for the infilling of My glory.

What is My glory? As you grow, joying in simple realizations of My fatherhood and of My love for My child, your anticipation of divine will in your life brings glory upon you.

Others will be led to witness your change, your growth from a child to a spirit of maturity, and in their desire to know the source of your strength I will be known.

You need not worry that you must have answers to be given or that perfection is expected of you or your character. No one wishing to grow spiritually would be charmed by another's perfection in concern that perfection is inaccessible to them. They instead, are given hope that they, too, are within the scope of possibilities for spiritual development.

It is Mine to cause to grow. It is Mine to plant those along the path who will teach, nurture and guide. And there are My angels whose guards are yours to keep you safe from your avengers.

Harvest Of Blessings

What I have spoken in the past I now bring to your attention in the way of things I would have you do for Me. You are chosen to deliver messages of hope to many left empty or barren. Those of you with treasures must lay them down and see what among them should be disbursed, shared. Many times those things that you feel need thinning out, those things that need discarding are the very things that could turn into joy for another.

Choose also from your storehouse some gift of the heart, that thing that you could not bear to release before. You will gain freedom in this giving if your heart is humbled and thereby happy in the giving of it.

Which of your possessions are treasures that bring glory to you or your house? Which are valued for what they say about you? Be careful what is said. Be careful what you say that may bring into being some harmful reality.

There are words that may become treasures in the heavenly realm. They are the words of a wise and faithful follower. God gives opportunity for these words to produce a harvest of blessings on earth and a heavenly reward as well. With a word given comes the responsibility that it be wrapped in love.

Pray to grow in love. Pray for wisdom in utterance.

Higher Ground

Come in obedience to hear the Word of the Lord. A discipline is required much as discipline meets the duties of each day and calls them done. It is I, your Lord, who call you to this task. Calling, I cajole, promise, entreat you in ways you would enjoy to hear My voice.

Yes, I know it is a hard task I call you to. But it is a task for which you have been prepared and made ready. This is not some frivolous plan newly conceived. I have had My host of angels digging the trenches that you may walk on higher ground in My will.

Give thanks that you are never alone in the task to which you are called. Indeed, give thanks for My helpers who have strived on your behalf. Be thankful, too, that your gifts are sufficient for the task even as I am sufficient to provide all you need for its accomplishment.

Persevere

I say to persevere when things seem too difficult for human kind to bear. Persevere in praise, though praise seems out of place in such a time.

Don't you see beyond this veil to My holy gates? They are to be entered into with praise - praise and thanksgiving, for upon the wings of this praise your heart is borne to higher levels. Here you may find the hope that is needed in such a time.

Praise! In blessing Me you will receive a blessing.

Search Out New Places

So many things await your eyes' delight. Have they become dulled as with old age? It is your responsibility to look for, search out new places where I have placed My beauty. You could find new beauties to behold every day and live your life without discovering all I have to share with you.

It was My joy to create intricacies and simplicities for sometimes no other reason than to delight Myself. As I continue to delight in them it becomes My delight to unfold them unto you.

Mourning Into Praise

Do not think that because the earth has used her gifts for foolish and irresponsible gains that I leave you only to bear that guilt. There are still gifts and treasures that I choose to hold in which you may delight.

Praise Me for the treasures that you see now. The pounding feet of the rhinoceros is a drumbeat for your dance of praise. Turn your mourning into praise which becomes the laughter of our hearts in unity.

Ask, Then Listen

Understand that the plan is much larger than what consumes your daily thought.

Remember the God of your childhood? He was a mighty presence that filled the sky when you looked up to find Him. He was more than a face in the clouds. He was the clouds.

I am still a mighty presence capable of holding all the cares of the world in My hands. I hold these cares and I plan for their comfort and healing.

Ask what you may do on a greater scale to alleviate the cares of the world. Ask. Then listen with your heart to My response.

Pray For My Anointing

You must have your leaders as well as your poets. My servant, David, was a warrior and a musician, a shepherd of lambs, and he was also a king.

Few are so anointed with such visions of glory in which they may be used so mightily. A song of the Lord may be a mighty weapon of war and also a melody of praise. It is My anointing which makes this a gift of power and of grace.

Imagine! Both power and grace, authority and sensitivity invested in the same anointing. I choose whom I choose on whom to bestow these blessings. These blessings carry the responsibility for their use, and I must be included in that plan and action for divine will to accomplish its purpose.

Pray for My anointing according to your ability and according to divine wisdom. Then pray daily to operate in fullest measure of their infilling.

Throne Of Grace

Lay to rest the burdens of past sins which you have asked Me to forgive. You do well to bring them to Me as I have charged them to your ledger. But hear Me when I tell you that through My son Jesus, your sins died upon that cross.

Is there some pleasure rejoiced in that makes you bring them up again? Do you miss the stench of their demise? You give them new life every time you drag up their remains.

Purge yourself once and at last from the memory of such a thing. When doubt or regret puffs up that thought, come to the throne of grace and receive again My mercy. My mercy and My grace are sufficient. In them you may walk in newness of life.

A Thank Offering

You are tempted in times of grief over the loss of someone you love to seek that person's face and to hear some words of consolation.

What will make your burden lighter? What will ever release death's grip upon your heart? My angels, My servants come to comfort you.

Prepare your life so that each day is a thank offering for the gift of that life shared. I entrusted him to you for you had what was needed for his journey.

I, too, am sorry for your pain, but I am thankful that you elected to experience it in the face of embracing love.

Rest In My Presence

Yes, My plan for your salvation includes a joy unspeakable if you will turn again and again to the treasures of My word.

When you wonder where the newness has gone spend time alone with Me. When another has dashed your spirit upon the rocks, turn to Me and give yourself the time, stilling your mind and heart in My presence. I will come to lead you beside still waters where you may be refreshed.

You do not need mountaintops of halleluia praises to come to a place of peace. I tell you, rest in My presence. No subjugation is necessary, no pleading to make your inmost cries be heard.

I am within. My Holy Spirit does My bidding on your behalf with all intentions of love, caring and consolation. Trust Me to respond to your needs. It is My delight to love you so.

Experience Life!

I teach you as you become capable of learning. No lesson is as costly as the one which requires your commitment to Me. In asking you to die to things of the world I ask you to experience Life! Life as it was given to God's children in the beginning.

This life is not free from harassment nor is it plagued with discontent. But commitment to it, to Me, is a keepsafe from death in this realm and beyond.

Do I mean that life is forever? That you will go from entity to entity, existence to existence?

There are limitations which still are in order with the universe. Honor this order as coming from the Father of all the universe and seek to live in His presence.

An Uplifting Of Spirit

Even My closest servants, My dearest children come to need an uplifting of spirit. I understand how hard it becomes to live in happy expectation or joyfulness. Your life on earth is crossed, by necessity, with the marks of others' tracks.

You ask, "What can I do to keep afloat, to keep my chin above the rising tide of pain and unknowing?"

Find a glade wherein My secrets of nature work their healing flow. Take your thoughts away from self-examination, from self-pity. Turn them to the simple delights that I will show you.

Lay your cares at My feet. Lay them there for My mending. Leave them there and go about your tasks as I go about Mine to heal and restore.

You say you want out of that arena where I have placed you? It is too hard. It is too difficult to keep yourself clean and pure of thought.

It is true that I have placed you among many of moral corruption whom I desire to be free from sins of lust and perversions. I do hear your call to be free from their influence.

Remember that I have placed My angels all about you to foresee any dart that would penetrate your armor. Yes, they have been working without rest to keep you in My will even though your walk is pocked with holes.

I have given you a love for these of Mine around whom I place you, these who now cause you to want to run. The battle is sometimes hardest just before victory. It still is My battle. I still call to them to return to Me, their Father God. I still can use you in that place.

Hold on. Hold on to Me as I walk beside you in these days of trial. Keep your focus on My works in the kingdom. There is justice ahead for those who lead My people astray, who call them to betray Me.

Now pray. I hear your prayers and prepare release for your burdens.

Share With Me

You have learned about stewardship as well as discipleship. I am removing the hindrances that you may share with Me the wealth of blessings of My Father's inheritance.

Doors To My Temple

Because you invite Me into your work and into your work place, I honor you with My presence there. You may know without doubt that I desire to work alongside you bringing your best to the task. It is I who give you love (and sometimes the mere tolerance) for these you touch each day. I use you in ways unsuspected by you that doors be opened to My temple.

Now I ask you, come to work with Me. I will be honored by your presence.

A Different Call

There are those of Mine who have yet to call Me Abba, Father. As I desire, the Holy Spirit seeks to inspire some working or wooing to call them in.

A different call is given, a harp or a whistle, a drum or violin, the cry of a bird or of a baby. Each may bring to mind a power greater, more majestic or humble for explaining mysteries.

I will open doors to My kingdom that you may not suspect, for I am ever clearing the path to lead Mine own to Me.

My Checklist

Think of it! These days on earth are work days that determine eternal rewards! Your tasks on earth well done, deserve also an earthly reward, and I have promised to provide for your needs in all things.

Stay in My presence. Let your work be guided by the checklist I give you. Be ready at a moment's notice to change directions if I ask you. Be ready to say, "Show me the next step. I am ready."

There is a labor of love. Your commitment to the job I lay out for you is a love in which I am pleased. With this love comes a reward to justify the sweat of your brow.

Seeds In Your Larder

There is a time of harvest and a time of storing up that which has been harvested. It is Mine to choose the ripest wheat as well as the barren fields for next year's crop.

I prepare the list of next year's planting and I foresee the needs of the ground that must be prepared. As much must go in to make it ready there are farmers who come to the task as I lead them.

Sow according to the seeds placed in your larder. Prepare, plan for the planting that many be filled with its bounty.

Change Is Required

The time now is going to be difficult, but you have entrusted to My care the people in need of My washing and preparation for use.

Change is required and you must not rescue and thereby preclude the resulting turmoil. It is necessary to bring all out that must come to the surface for revelation and therefore, for cleansing.

Remember your time of confrontation? Although painful, the well had to be dug free of the mud that had sifted in and settled there before the water could run clear.

I call you to drink of cool, clear water. I call you to be refreshed. The time is coming when you may sit by the well and drink.

That Unseen World

Oh, children! Please listen to the cries all around you. You are not the only ones seeking justice or liberation from the powers that hold you captive. Remember that the battle is in that unseen world, and it is a battle for your very soul.

Be sure that your allegiance is with Me, your Father God, the Creator of the very universe that is the battleground. Your foes come to take My loved ones away from Me. Do they understand that the greatest punishment is to experience the absence of love?

Let this be a lesson to you: *be* the presence of love for someone. Practice this love. Make it something you do, and this doing may be simply sitting at the side of one in need.

Ask to be shown how to express in word and deed this love.

Divine Offerings

Your labor is not without its reward. You labor with your hand and with the abilities given unto you. I may choose to labor within the span of your gifts unseen. That is the ripple effect of the work you are doing.

If I have blessed you with a work to do no matter how simple or what may seem unprofitable in the kingdom, do not doubt that I am using it and you for the working of divine offerings to others.

What I call worthy others may not recognize as worthy. What I call holy may seem to others to be ordinary. What others call of the spirit may in fact emanate from the core of self and not from My spirit, which is indeed holy.

Go about the labor before you searching My Word each day to prove this which I have told you. Seek Me and I will use you and your labor. This is your commission: seek ye the kingdom of God and all these things shall be added to you.

Conflict Of The Soul

Not by might, not by power, but by the Spirit of the Lord! This is what saves man from things both secret and subtle. What you cannot see and what you are unaware of in the spirit world may be the very thing that seeks the destruction of My good will for your life.

These things are not within the scope of your understanding or your vision. The enemy plans your seduction with the desires of your heart in mind. He seeks to gain entry into the very heart of your being by claiming some weakness as a thing to be desired. When you feel yourself drawn by just the breadth of a thought into a conflict of the soul there is a choice to be made. It remains your free will, the Father's gift to you, to choose.

You can be sure that a host of angels awaits your decision. They stand at the ready to do the Father's bidding on your behalf. You will not have to bear the burden alone, but will yourself, be borne up on angel wings with this decision won to overcome your temptation.

Pray For Deliverance

Remember that Satan appears as an angel of light. His dark angels also await your decision.

Pray for deliverance. Call the name of Jesus Christ. In that name your victory is assured. Call His name, Jesus, the Hope, the Consolation, the Strength for this moment.

Seek the Lord and rest in Him and He will purify the desires of your heart. It is His good will to delight you with many blessings.

Walking Midst The Fire

Victory shouts with the masses and whispers with the weak of heart, "I have overcome!"

And overcome, you shall, for it is by My design that a page of history turns before the end is written for all to rejoice. All rejoice that is, except those of darkness who have had to pick up their snares and carry them to some other battleground.

I have prepared a victory for you in this very hour, in this very battle that rages around you. Remember that as the three were released from walking midst the fire that not even their hair smelled of the flames that sought to consume them!

Healing Comes

You guard your heart because of the hurt that has made you vulnerable. I come now to heal these past hurts if you will lay them down before Me. Lay them down and refuse to pick them up again.

Bring these who have caused the hurt before Me. Leave them here. And when you are tempted to think of them and this hurt, come again into My presence lifting them up for My healing and forgiveness.

Yes, they, too, need healing and they need your prayers. Your healing is not contingent upon theirs or upon your bringing them before Me. Your healing comes as your heart grows closer to Me in love and forgiveness.

A Realm Beyond

As long as the body has breath in it there is hope that I may come to rescue and save that one from the sure eternal death without Me. There is a realm beyond the conscious awareness in which I may move and breathe new life.

Never lose hope that it is not too late for My grace to administer its healing balm upon one so in need. I, too, long to bathe away the the tears and give newness of life.

Abundance

Open your heart and your mind to things I am now bringing to you. You have learned how important it is to receive, and I have planned your progress with this in mind.

There is bountiful abundance within your reach. Yes, you shall bless others upon the way to receiving it. Your heart has confessed its envy of the fortune of others. You have laid before Me your displeasure in your own covetousness.

Because your heart is sincere I have forgiven you and have planted new seeds of joy for others. I have also planned good things for your pleasure and abundance that you will delight in sharing.

Growth And Prosperity

Sit before Me, and when all has been said that is on your heart, sit before Me. Can you imagine a king's court with the suppliant waiting, waiting on the king's response? Does he feel anxious, fear before this one of authority? Awe in the presence of royalty?

As you sit before Me I would have you know the assurance of My wisdom in responding to you. As I have formed you, I also have planned your growth and with it, your prosperity.

Yes, prosperity does mean blessings of a financial nature. But prosperity also means treasures that may be stored up for your use in the heavenly realm where you will spend eternity.

I Am

Who would call Me Blessed would also call Me Supreme above all other spirit gods.

"I Am" is My name and is My description of My work before the world began. "I Am" says what you cannot possibly behold, as no other goes before Me to discern this truth. You, too, are called to purpose and this uttering is a cry and a desire to be acknowledged both here and especially, beyond.

"I Am" counts the days when those who have forever turned to lesser gods must at last turn and say, "Father God, the great I Am. Beside you there is no other."

Receive Grace

That one who has given you much misery is now in need of forgiveness. Not because he deserves your forgiveness do I ask it of you. Not because he even recognizes his sin and misdeeds against you do I ask for mercy on his behalf. He is lost to My blessings as one who has forever lived in blind submission to the rise and fall of life's current.

You are the child much loved who has had the comfort and knowledge of security within My house. You have had the assurance of provision for your needs through lack or plenty.

He has had himself, fed himself, looked always over his shoulder through good or adversity. His reward is only himself with which he may leave this world.

I ask you to have mercy. If you will but ask Me to supply the source for this, to fill your being with limitless compassion I am quick to give you what is required. The supply for all you need to be a loving, faithful servant is within My ability to give.

Soften your heart to receive grace that My mercy be poured out in full measure.

Lightness Of Heart

All is not a serious study. All is not deep contemplation of My will for each of your steps. There is joy to be found in a lightness, too, of heart. I wish this for you to experience contentment in your life.

Go with a happiness that says, I am satisfied that today holds goodness. Expect that it will overtake your journey. There is much to be found and to be shared.

A New Refreshing

My land is ready for the plowing in of human concern. It has been tilled and sown, tilled and sown until new soil is needed to replenish it with nutrients.

Look at the weariness of her people who labor without the rewards of past days. A new refreshing is needed that they may lift their heads, that their eyes may behold the promise and the hope of rest from their labor.

I did not always call My children from the fields before the harvest was gathered. But My children need a refreshing, too, new hope that indeed, I am working to produce plenty for their reward.

Lift your voice in praise, lift your hands to show honor that God is keeper of His vineyard and purveyor of all who work in His fields.

Restoration

Strength, that filling into the body and also into the spirit, that strength is but a part of My provisions for your dark night. I have allowed the waning of your strength while I also keep guard to ensure that you are not lost to despair.

I do not receive joy at your pain or your weakness. Instead, I send out more to fight for you, more to shield you against further onslaught of the dark. These servants of love within My realm are going forth with your victory in mind.

What you will learn during this process will bind your wounds in days to come. You will be restored by the knowledge that you gave as much as was available for your giving.

I ask you, take only the step that is before you. Leave the second task until the first has been completed. In this way you may be assured that each is accomplished as it unfolds.

I make you capable of fulfilling what is required. Do your part, keeping in mind the desire of others to be a part of the healing process.

My Suffering Servants

The time is coming, is even here when My presence will be made known to these you love who befriend you as you, even you have needed.

Yes, I, too, have needed them to love you and I have used them to show you a more perfect way of My loving nature. In this way by My hand and in My mercy I bring each of you to My side.

Do not question or worry that the gate will be closed to My suffering servants. Remember what I told you of that one who carries the Word throughout his daily work by the things he does and says to help? It is this conveyance that marks one as My servant.

I will speak to the heart. You are to be faithful to My witness in sometimes the smallest way, the quietest moment, the softest touch.

My Holy Spirit has a duty to fulfill, that of conveying a mighty power, a wind of change blowing away clouds of confusion and ill-formed thoughts.

You are to pray without ceasing for these whom I love, whom I have called to serve you as you minister to them. It is My joy to lead them unto Me by the words I give you.

Trust them to My care. Thank you for loving them.

The Battle Rages

Mighty warriors are now being readied for the battle to win lost souls to Me. It will require many to defeat the forces, increasing, increasing in number in Satan's army.

I foresaw this day and this battle. I also foresaw the victory as it was given to My people and My land.

I hate losing even one to the foe but that one has made his decision to follow unrighteousness. He has chosen to remain angry, vindictive, full of acts of vengeance. The cheek he would turn has instead been the jaw jutted out with the pride of sin. Humility has been a curse word to him. He has chosen the world's glory rather than the peace of reconciliation.

Now the battle rages and he must take up his sword again. You will feel the heat of his anger as you stand in My campground. You will experience a tiredness of heart as you carry the arms of a peacemaker. This is inevitable.

Inevitable, too, is victory for My overcomers, My peacemongers. You will thrill when the last cry of the battle is a shout throughout the land of victory.

Look to Me as your Power, your Intercessor, your Avenger. Stand firm. I give you strength for the day and rest for the night.

Darkness Comes

Listen when I say that darkness comes as a thief in the night to carry away any who have not prepared or guarded their treasures.

This darkness is deceit let loose in the world to seek its harvest of foolish and stubborn people.

I have been with you as you asked for other gods, other diadems. I have stood by watching your hope become disappointment as your gods became only too human in nature.

You are to learn of My omnipotence, that even in this power I choose to give you freedom to search every corner of space itself for one greater than I.

Yet, I wait...the real test of power, for waiting allows time for learning, searching, and the growing in spirit that may lead you back to Me. It is important that you come to Me out of your own desire to know who I am. Ask Me. I long to reveal to you My truths.

Tempest Of Indecision

The day is darkest wherein reigns the tempest of indecision. You have heard it said that God is not the author of confusion. What, then, can become of one so torn that neither right nor left beckons? Truly he is tossed about on that stormy sea waiting to be thrown upon the sand of any nation or thought that would give him home.

There is a quiet place within where you may rest. Go there and stay until peace settles your thoughts. If you invite Me to sit with you I will not refuse you or your need of counsel.

A friend is a valued companion for such times as these. I am your friend.

My Vision For You

You have found what I told you is true: I have worked out the solution even before you began tossing your own answers about.

Your prayer partner who was so readily available is only one of the ones I will use to bring peace to your challenges. That one told you, "God writes His desire on your heart."

As you discover the wonder, the pure delight in My vision for your life, I, too, delight that you have persevered to the point of conquest.

Golden Arrows

Just as quickly as you are ready will I respond. It is your pace that determines Mine. And I am ever eager to quicken the pace that you may continue onward, higher and higher to the mark set before you.

I do know that change is hard. Change is frightening. You risk leaving the familiar behind heading for the unknown. It is harder, still, when you have not yet learned that to depend on Me is to feel secure in your decisions.

I hold good things in My hand for you. They are like a quiver of arrows made ready and put into the bow one at a time. If an arrow fails to hit its mark it is possible to find it, take aim once again, and pull back the bow string with more precision and more accuracy.

Think of the challenges before you as golden arrows. Then see how I project you forward as timing and preparation allow.

The Supernatural

Mighty in deed! That is what men shall say as I reveal Myself more and more. They will stand in awe, "Behold!

What miracles are surrounding these who walk in the footsteps of the holy God."

Many false teachers, false prophets and seducing spirits continue performing acts to call you away from truth and into their kingdom of mysticism. I have not restrained their power to work in the supernatural even though it is within My rights and My agencies to call them down.

The test of righteousness is the same as it has been down the ages: Whom do you say the Son of Man is?

More than a teacher, more than a prophet, more than a miracle worker, He is My Son sent to earth in all the frailties and strengths of your human form.

Call on Me when doubts threaten. Your Father leads you to a path of truth and gives you light for the way.

My Saints

There is a striving within the company of prophets over who shall be most pure. This too, is an abomination. It leads to decay of a solid foundation.

Where there is division whether in the body of the saints or elsewhere, there is weakness open to decay. Yes, My saints are subject to being pulled into unrighteousness. They have not reached perfection nor have they the eyes of holiness.

I call Mine saints who daily commit themselves to Me and My kingdom. They continue to grow in spiritual understanding and concepts. It is necessary that this growth process begins on earth that a place be made ready to receive them in the greater sphere of My abiding.

When one falters, when one falls to temptation that is so readily, humanly available, have mercy upon that one as even you would have need of mercy at such a time.

I am teaching you about My saints. I am holding them before you that they be not either revered on earth as holy or disdained as contemptible weaklings. You, too, are called to sainthood. I do not have contempt for your failures but honor the desire of your heart to grow in My likeness.

Learn Of The Holy Spirit

Yes, many await the downfall of what they determine to be the hypocrisy of ordered religion. Their hurts, their experience confirms what is reality to them: that the only justice is that which they themselves mete out.

There have been misunderstandings throughout the history of religious attempts at conversion. Man has misinterpreted his challenge from God to bear His standard as an instruction to bear arms against any who disagree.

How many have been pushed aside by the pride of human error, by the condemnation of one seeking power or control in the name of God? Did they consider that it is freedom that I offer? Did they feel for themselves this freedom of choice, freedom from restraints of past sins and debts now forgiven?

Be soon to look upon the conformities of religion as man's attempt in all he understands to order things of the spirit. There is godliness in order. There is familiarity and a dependable source of comfort.

Turn your heart and mind to the Spirit, itself. Learn of the Holy Spirit the true things of God. I long to give you freedom that only My mercy and My grace offer.

Simplicity And Purity

You say that what you need now is divine inspiration. Your plans have all come to a dead end. Your hopes have no wings nor a place on which to land.

Sometimes the most obvious idea or thought, the one rejected because it seemed impossible, impractical is that one in need of consideration. You have become consumed by the business of daily living. Being consumed leaves no room for creative thought.

Instead of falling to despair, instead of fixing blame use this opportunity as a time of direction not a time of void. You must spend time alone with Me and learn to hear My voice.

Perhaps you think that you do not have time for letting Me speak into your dreams and visions. I say that you do not have time to waste shuffling in the dust of the work world. It is impeding your sight.

You are to learn patience in this trial. Don't become angry at the marketplace where others have found their home/work. All avenues are necessary to access all levels of growth, need, and accomplishment.

Consider the lilies of the field. They toil not, neither do they spin. Yet I have clothed them in beauty. I also know your needs. Look to Me, ask for My provisions, seek My will in all things. You will in this way be drawn to My voice and My wish for you. I desire a path of simplicity and purity for you, one which will delight you and in which you will rejoice to be so used.

So Great A Burden

You have expected that your hard work would garner rewards of heavenly value, your good deeds marks of favor. If this were so I would not have born so great a burden on the cross for you. The debts for your sin and pain I paid on the hill of Golgotha.

There are others whose sins remain a heavy weight upon their weary backs. Yet, My back was sufficient to carry them all. The tears I shed were in shared sorrow for their grief. Pouring out My blood was not without pain because of who I am, God on earth. Indeed, because I was God-Man and Am, My pain for you continues.

I will not cause some tragedy to bring you to your knees that I may rescue you. It is not within the being of My nature to set the stage for tragedy in your life.

Whom Will You Serve?

Oh, mortal man, is not this the time of your accountability? Is not this the time of your recompense?

What you have sown will be looked upon for its merit in the spiritual world. What will you hold up as your offering of forgiveness? Is your present sorrow a divining rod to the seat of mercy? Are your regrets worthy of placing on the altar of sacrifice?

Mourn and weep. There comes this time now when you can no more look to your own power to be made pure. You have seen your own constraints and limitations. You have reached into the darkness of other realms for guidance and help.

Still, you are not satisfied. There is still an unanswered question: whom will you serve? I am a jealous God who longs to love you with the love you have sought and desired. When you decide to come to Me you will find My arms outstretched for you. You will find that your heart no longer aches with empty yearning. You will find the forgiveness that wipes clean your record of the past.

Find this newness of life in Me. I wait for you, long for your presence with Me for all eternity. I have made the sacrifice for all your debts. What other God has loved you so?

Pride of Self-Sufficiency

When you begin to find that your answers are empty vessels still looking for fulfillment you begin to understand the lesson of humility. You begin looking at the pride of self-sufficiency.

Humble yourself and begin to find a new way of living, a way of real courage and true blessings.

To any who would come I stand ready to bear your burdens and lift you into the presence of the Holy God. It is His love which offers forgiveness and refreshing hope where had been poverty and deprivation of spirit.

My joy is to have suffered all the pain of humanity that you might have a way out of earthly bonds and into the freedom of reconciliation with your Creator.

Lay down your burden. I have borne it for you.

Sorrowful Goodbyes

Begin to release that one who faintly hears My voice calling, "Come home." I wish it weren't so painful for you to let go. It is helpful that you understand that the next step allows glorious entrance into My kingdom. I understand your wanting to cling to your loved one even though his life there is fragile.

It is not that your understanding is lacking but that your need is to hold on. Ask yourself whose need would require that one to stay. If the need is yours list those things which you must do to free yourself of them.

Do you need to express your love? Ask forgiveness? Spend time? Offer forgiveness? Mend some hurt? Taking care of any of these does not preclude sorrowful goodbyes. It will, however, give you both grounds for rejoicing in days to come.

My Emissaries

The Lord your God awaits. Although within My power to compel a turning of the clock in favor of a quick and just response, I wait. My understanding and My patience save you from the pit of dark confusion you have chosen. I must watch as you struggle to work out your own resolutions. I grieve that you cannot see beyond the web you have spun.

My ear is turned to hear your softest utterance for divine help. There are many ways that I may send rescue, many people who care and may be My emissaries.

Drop your cloak of superiority. Become as one who stands in need and is open to the help and, thereby, the love of others. It is a way of offering love to lend a hand at such a time.

Have you not heard that God is Love?

Source Of Power

The tide of men's actions has a determinable source of power. Its resulting effect upon the world is an expression of that source.

You may not feel that you can affect world powers or change their source of strength. But your influence within your circle of knowledge and friendship will no doubt echo from one to one to one with resounding effects.

See that the tide in your life has as its source a power unfettered by human desires and illusions.

System Of Accounting

Forgiveness...consider what this means: to erase a debt, to cease to resent. In that light you must look differently upon that one you say you have forgiven. Is there still resentment that you were so treated?

When I look back on your record of the past I see no check beside deeds to remind Me of your shame. Can you say the same of your record book?

I will show you how to put aside your system of accounting, to replace it with a clean sheet. Be willing to forgive and these things you think impossible to forgive or forget I take into My own accountability. I am just. I mete out and garner what is necessary for each of you to have victory.

The ability to forgive and the ability to seek forgiveness are within My power to give. Ask for My righteousness in all things.

Anticipation

Many people are satisfied to have before them simply the plans for a day. Yet you wonder what joy can be found without something to hope for, something on which the future relies.

I know you find contentment in so many of My blessings on any given day. I know you delight in simplicities unnoticed but by a few.

I do not find you disrespectful. But I do keep ever before you tasks to feed your interests, to hone your abilities, to bring you to a place of anticipation, yes, anticipation of each day as I give it to you. When the time is right for preparing a larger scene for your palette, you will be able to look at it in its incompleteness and you will rejoice in its unfolding, day by day by day.

New Challenges

A decision is called for. You may either gather facts and ask for prayer help concerning them, or you may make the decision by default. That is, you ignore the available information until the time for deciding passes you by.

Even though I have given you promises to order your steps if you put your trust in Me, the process is not easy. Trust is not easy especially when life experiences don't reflect the trustworthiness of people and situations.

I must tell you that I am not like those who have betrayed you. I am faithful to keep My promises, to provide whatever is necessary for your journey.

Don't lose hope or become discouraged with new challenges so close at hand.

Be Assured

Mighty in truth, mighty in spirit, mighty in works! This is the God who also loves in gentle admonition and with abundant grace.

You will not understand the complexities of your God. But be assured that all you need to understand about Him and His workings He will open to you. He will open to you in ways that are so beautiful and so precise to your particular way of acceptance that you will be astounded in their presentation.

The Bridge

With the answering for the present time the questions that had you rushing to be sure your obligation in the matter was satisfied, you now may return to the work at hand.

Any avenue that requires you to cross it so hurriedly that you cannot look both ways is an avenue that may lead to a dead end. I afford lessons as so described, but it is not My intention that you be fraught with confusion.

I understand your need of companionship, a fellowship of equality and trust. When I had the host of the animal world to comfort and befriend Me I nevertheless lacked companionship that man was purposed to fill.

Your most trusted friend is one who shares the intimacy of prayer. It is not that they have shared interests in family or work or play. It is that they have a desire to plead with you your concerns before the heavenly Father. This is a love on which a bridge may be built to see you safely to the other side of the avenue.

Work Of Art

Turn that situation around when you find yourself wondering what purpose that other one has in your life. You might say, "Why has God sent me to them? Show me the need, Lord, that I may be used for Thy purpose."

It is true that I cross your path with some who are willing to be used by Me to aid your circumstances. If you fail to notice that My desire is to use you, too, you miss the best growth lesson and sometimes the best gift.

I find in those willing to serve a pliability of which the most intricate of sculptures may be molded. The artwork they are willing to become was not conceived, prepared, or perfected without much trial. Even then its perception sometimes required the stepping back and viewing in different light.

Much bending, shaping and agonizing tears beget a pure, unblemished work of art. Some have recognized such a one as a true Masterpiece.

Mankind In Unison

What a glorious day will be that day of My transformation. I will be released to work freely among My chosen. No longer will I be restrained from healing and blessing, and from casting aside the stumbling blocks to My work.

Move quickly now to prepare yourself. Pray to be used in the preparation of others as well. Many are lost and know nothing of My glory, so how could they possibly look with anticipation at the day of My reconciliation with the earth? Will they be forced to say, "Why has no one told me? Why was this great truth hidden from me?"

I do rely on My message bearers to spread the news of My coming glory and of their position on that day. My greatest joy would be to see all mankind in unison before Me. The song they will sing no ear has ever heard, no thought has ever imagined.

And no rejoicing has ever resounded throughout all eternity as will be on that day when My people join the holy throng in one voice of praise. Go out with the message of My return to claim victory over death and all things unholy. Let it be said by no one, "I didn't know."

Be Shored Up

Do not worry that your call lands on deaf ears. It is the work of the Holy Spirit to see that that one is prepared to receive My Word. He also will appoint the time and content of your speaking.

Your responsibility is to be shored up with words and knowledge from the heart of the Father. Your responsibility is to keep yourself pure in His sight. You must have a well from which to draw. The water cannot be polluted so that you do not contaminate without from contamination within.

Trust that even in that time when you are unaware of My intent to use you, I will guard your tongue. When you become as familiar with My voice as are My sheep, nothing will escape the opportunity I give to reach one in need of My word, My hand.

The Chamber Room

Blessed are the poor in spirit. Yes, they shall see God. That means that their search is to fill every part of their existence with that spirit that is God himself, that spirit that is Love, that spirit that is Mercy upon all people and all creatures. That is God.

For one to be so humble as to ask for more and more of God's presence, his very awareness of his incompleteness leads to the door and into the chamber room of the holy God.

He acknowledges, I am of no good thing without the spirit of the Lord. In that poor confession he is not condemned, but is lifted to behold the majesty that is God.

Quest For Knowledge

Who is this God who calls forth the creation of worlds and makes the way for stars to burst upon the heavens? Is He a traveler of spheres? A force of divine or cosmic energy? Is it He who climbed the spiral of spiritual evolution to its highest stage?

I rejoice at your quest for knowledge. It was My intent to give you the joys of learning and the keys to unfold mysteries.

You must be aware that the first man and woman were also desirous of the knowledge of all things. Yet, their price paid exacted a burden the weight of which the world continues to bear.

Do you think My thoughts are too simple to challenge your intellect? Am I without understanding of your capacity to develop and expand? Would I choose to control your path, your quest for spiritual enlightenment? Put Me to the test. See if I am not worthy to be called God.

A Personal God

I am a personal God. I understand your innermost thoughts that cannot be shared with others. I do walk beside you in the day of darkness when you are in need of loving companionship. I bear your sorrow as no other can. And at those times when you are alone and your heart is made to laugh at simple pleasures, I am pleased at your joy.

There is no other who shares your triumphs or your agony with equal understanding of the steps that led you there. Your victories are also Mine and I dance with you in celebration. Your defeats I accept as does a father wishing away the pain.

Yet, I am able to go one further step by taking all the elements of its design, changing each as though molecule by molecule so that the end result brings a good and profitable thing.

If you knew how available I am you would come to Me in assurance of My arms outheld to you. When I tell you that I come as your friend, trust My worthiness to be called your friend. When I say I understand each and every need, I separate your wants out of them to be sure your provisions are for your good. Are these not the considerations of a personal God?

Seek Communion

You are right in thinking that you must change in order to be a more useful vessel. Though I may use My committed servants at any time there is cause I can more readily call upon one who is not only yielded, but sanctified.

In this sanctification, this lifting up before the Light you must be willing to own even the thoughts with which you condemn one of My children. It is My judgment that person brings to himself, and where in that realm is your judgment of value? It, thereby, turns from judgment upon another to condemnation upon yourself.

Pray without ceasing. Always seek communion with Me. I will be sure to guide your changes if you will let Me open your eyes to that need. Pray for humility before Me and I will show you humility before the world. It is this humbleness of heart that reconciles to Me a world hardened with pain and anger.

Gifts and Abilities

The Lord your God who made you and knows you by part and in whole, yearns, yes, longs for the fulfilling of every gift and ability instilled into your nature.

With your attention attuned to hear My urging, "Go here, speak to that one, wait and abide for a while" I am able to call into purpose for you those things prepared for your advancement.

There must sometimes be a struggle for you in following My plan. The world still desires to appeal to you on every front, enticing you through your senses as well as through your intellect.

Turn again to Me and if you must, wait there until you are sure of My guiding. Abide until My peace enters and surrounds you.

Do not fear that in calling upon My guidance you will be limited in developing your full capabilities. That seed I planted in you I will also water and cause to flower. Stay close to Me and the fruit you were designed to bear will grow in abundance.

Forsake Illusions

Only I am able to present you before the Father of the heavens, blameless and purified. Only I am concerned that you be made fit for presentation to Him who is waiting for His perfect bride.

Do not be distracted by tempting spirits who call you good, or healer of men, or worshipper of the spirits of the universe, or walker among angels.

What a tragedy you experience if you stray into these heavens without My mark upon your head, without My name upon your heart!

Your questions regarding these things are answerable only in time. Should you demand their answer now you walk without faith in the omnipresent, omnipowerful purpose and will of the Most High God.

Use your time there wisely. Come humbly before Me and let Me speak to your heart the answers to divine questions. Learn of the Holy Spirit the mysteries of the heart and breath of divine and godly communion.

You cannot worship spirits of the universe and also worship the God who is supreme above them.

In all things, all things I will move mountains for the perfecting of your spirit. Ask for this. Forsake the path of illusions and come to the solid walk of trust in the God of all creation. He will reveal Himself as the true Lover of your soul.

Men and Angels

Many times I decry the making of My own hands. But when men and angels are eager to hear and obey I find solace in their delight of Me.

Not only do I call upon them for My work to be done. I also send them, touch them, and cause them to touch others so that their own purpose may be fulfilled. This gives Me pleasure.

I walk upon the earth seeking those who know Me not. Who will walk with Me as I point out the needs of those whose healing is in My hand?

Learn of my Love that your heart be melted with passion for My work.

Close the Gap

You are now beginning to hear My voice. As you hear, say to yourself, "What is it that God would have me do?" Pay attention to the disquieting feelings, the indecisive agitation.

Is all not right? Is there something you need to do, something you need to change, something you need to say to make things right? These simple considerations may be all that is required to close the gap in a relationship. Be willing to take the first step for healing.

Whatsoever Is Lovely

Whatsoever is pure, whatsoever is lovely, whatsoever is admirable, if anything is excellent or praiseworthy, think about such things. Philippians 4:8, GNB.

Your very thoughts color every aspect of life for you and for many others whose lives you affect.

Do not lose sight of the importance of daily contacts, both personal and of mere acquaintances. To do so could find you misguided by your own efforts at self-sufficiency, your pride at independence. By such valiant and stalwart striving there may come to you a poverty so complete as to nullify the worth of your accomplishments.

Think of the lives of others whose need is to see "whatsoever is lovely," and cause their eyes to be so lifted up. You are made to work in harmony with these. They are your treasures to be stored, your blessings with whom you may share eternity.

Cleansing of Memories

When you have been so mistreated as to hang your head in sorrow or shame I do not take your pain lightly as do some. Their own experiences may keep them from identifying with you for fear of awakening unresolved pain of their own.

Find a resting place. Find a helper who has been made free from past burdens and whose ministry is to help you, too, gain this freedom.

It is possible to have renewal in your thoughts, your emotions, and cleansing of your memories. It is possible to walk with head up facing any person or situation in serenity and with confidence.

Ask Me for deliverance from these things that have kept you bound and unable to progress. Pray for the help of one of My ministering saints. I hear your prayers. Now listen for My response.

Who Are Saints?

Who are My ministering saints? Your search for them is made easier by placing yourself where you suspect they may be found.

You may expect that they are recognizable by their status or standing. You may think a saint too lofty or inaccessible, too busy for your concerns.

I tell you a saint is one of My children who also struggles, one who lifts before Me each day's burdens, who prays, "Not my will, but Thine be done."

Study My Word

You have not studied My word as needed. You fail to draw on it and to withdraw from it its wisdom.

I ask you now, open your heart, open your eyes, for I have revelations for you. I want to speak to you as never before in revelations previously hidden from your understanding.

What a marvelous blessing I plan for you, but you must do as I say and open unto Me this avenue of instruction.

It Is Soon To Be

My instructions for you are to listen with your heart, see with your spirit, and speak when you have received that inner voice of My command.

This is not to be a daily line of communication for you to depend on. I must have you out and about doing your work among many people. You must determine to do well the job to which you are presently committed.

I will send you out with new messages and into new fields as they become ready. Keep working, never losing hope of My sudden appearance to you giving new directions, new tasks and new companions to share My work.

It is soon to be, this field work which, as of yet, is not open or available to you. I will do as I have promised, preparing you for that abundance of life experiences that you long for and which I delight to give you.

If at any time you draw away from My house or from seeking the guidance and company of the Holy Spirit you prolong the time that precludes the ingathering I plan for you.

I promise you new abilities, the joy of people to share them, and the love born of their melding.

The Verge of Boldness

The field that is to be plowed is before you. I speak more urgently than before. I call on these, My laborers who are eager to prepare the ground for the implanting.

The restlessness you now feel is My tugging at your heartstrings to begin. Go on about your work today and I will show you step by step how to prepare. It is exciting to know that you are standing on the verge of boldness in new fields I have designed for you to plow.

Dare to Care

Can you see others with My eyes? Can you feel the imprint on their hearts that their life lessons have pressed there? Who would ask to be the pain-bearer for others?

If you concentrate on your own life lessons and their painful mark it is true that no amount of love or strength can suffice to grant that you carry this again for someone else. It is not to be.

I do not ask that your experience parallel another's. The tears your heart cries for him say that you understand and care.

Dare to risk caring about the circumstance that brings one to your heart. Dare to put actions to your caring.

The Unique Gift

You ask that the desires of My heart be placed upon yours. Your own desires now seem scattered, a whirlwind of changes without direction. You no longer plead for this to be or for that dream to be fulfilled.

It is this place apart from preconceived ideas of your future that I have waited on. Into this place free of restrictive mindsets I may now come and plant My seeds. These seeds are new ideas for your work and growth. They hold an abundance of the treasures of My heart for you.

Yes, My heart is filled with good things for all My children. How I long to bless them all, to have each one receive the unique gift planned for his special use and joy. To have this abundance within My treasury is of no consolation to Me if I cannot pour it out in abundance on those I love.

Free Will

There is the fear from many who believe that there are attached to My gifts strings which keep them captive. Haven't they always been allowed free will to choose and to come and go at their own discretion?

It is no different once they come into My courtyard. The difference is, or can be, that receiving the gifts of the Father holds such awe as to transform the very desires that brought them there. No longer do they desire to leave the presence of the Royal King.

Such gracious love is the closest thing here on earth to that day of all days when the presence of God is eternal joy.

Newly Born in Freedom

The Lord your God calls from His temple to make the way known to all who would hear. He is evermore searching for that one whose heart is yet to come into submission.

This submission is not to be feared. The enemy would have you believe that submission to God means giving up power, losing personal identity or forsaking friends. The enemy purports that submission to God equals weakness, mindlessness and a future void of fun.

Look closely at this deception. The enemy describes the fear of his own heart at losing grasp of one newly born in freedom and light.

Highest Thoughts of God

Walk in quietness in these days of contemplation. Don't let the shadow of discouragement overtake you, for that gives power to the side of darkness. Your position should always be clear: "I know whom I believe, and He will set my path before me."

Have continuing faith in the highest thoughts of God to prevail for you. Having faith means you will not always understand the way of God's working. While you cannot see what lies ahead, you may be assured of the unfolding according to divine will.

The Father sees all things with clarity, the things that are pure and the things which work against that purity to distort and even to work harm against His children. As a father does, He also calls His children close to Him that his arms may encircle them.

There is rest to be found with your Father. Pray to live your life within His will for you so that this rest is accessible.

Faith Requires Practice

The Way of the Lord is of necessity an arduous trail hidden from the understanding of those who do not follow Him. Even my followers sometimes find it difficult to keep on the path. Answers may not come swiftly as desired, and tomorrow's steps are not opened before them until tomorrow.

It does require faith which is more than the parroting of a teacher or prophet. Faith requires the practice of it. It is a daily settling into a time for spiritual learning, for listening before the Lord, for quieting those things that distract from hearing the whispers of God.

As more and more is gained through the Word of God about the heart of God, a trust begins to grow.

Is it true that falling in love with someone involves getting to know them on an intimate level? Is it about trusting them with innermost secrets? Is this the building of faith in them? This is also true about the Father who desires to build an intimate, personal relationship with you.

How can you receive that with which your experience is unfamiliar? The same again is true. Learn all you can of Him. Open your heart to Him. Fix your thoughts upon Him. This is the beginning of trust, the establishing of faith in One who walks today's path with you and leads the way of tomorrow.

Dance Before Him

Dance and sing as you praise the Lord. Your praises are born up to the throne of God on such things. When you find it difficult to rejoice in this way, begin to lift your hands up to Him. Begin giving Him words to express your love.

Let the words stir an awakening of the joy within. Do your part to unleash what is hiding there and the angels will dance at your efforts to overcome your heaviness of heart.

What you can imagine in the way of the dance of angels is so small in comparison to that reality. They find their greatest expression of love to be in singing and in dancing in praise.

Who are these angels? Were they always spirits of heaven whose existence found purpose in dance? Are they those who continue in that realm their dance from life on earth? Are they unblemished, newborn souls, or are they forgiven converts from darkness, now free?

The Lord God receives the praise of those who so love Him as to dance before Him, who serve in heaven or on earth by rising up from the desire of their own hearts. The glory of the Lord shines around them.

Pass It On

Let the voice of him who loves the Lord be heard from generation to generation. Among those who are your closest in love, they are to be message receivers and, in turn, message bearers.

This may prove to be the hardest lesson, for in living day upon day with another you become closely attuned to both the despicable and the praiseworthy. Your traits, too, are thusly known.

Therefore, let it be told of you and your house that you are peace loving and given to kindness to each other. See that you are a servant in your own house first before you give yourself out to others.

What thing you desire most, whether it be acceptance, high standing, high regard, see that you offer it first, paying heed to those about you.

So live that in others may be seen a generosity of love placed there in your emulation.

God Is Spirit

Man enjoys a consciousness of spirit on earth and beyond that allows choices of the spirit, yet not allowing choices of existence, for he is not god. Man is not his own creator. But God, who is within him, continually longs for expression.

Is the substance of this God intellect? Wisdom? Source and provider? Can the spirit that is God be love at its core? Does love cause to purpose wise thought? Does love manifest provisions?

You have heard that God is love. You have heard that God is within you. With man, whose consciousness of spirit is capable of choices comes the decision for putting love in action.

Put yourself in touch with God who longs to express His creative love through you. God is spirit, and that spirit is love.

Do Not Be Deceived

Oh, that My world would quickly, now, turn from pleasures that do nothing to lift them, neither in character, spirit, or in happiness. That joy is but a false joy, a temporary ecstasy serving to confuse the issue of its origin.

It is written that God is not the author of confusion. Understanding that, it becomes difficult to consider who, then, is its author. Who, then, must claim responsibility for making room for confusion to enter?

My Way may not be fully understood. It may even seem to be unfair when following it calls for leaving friends or familiar excitements behind. I am sad when faced with anger from one I have welcomed into My kingdom. I am also patient and will offer My love all the more until My blessings upon that one are at last recognized, received, and acknowledged in true thanksgiving.

Journey of Adventure

Where I lead I also prepare you for the journey. The Israelites had with them on their wanderings people who could provide comfort and companionship. I made man to enjoy and learn from the company of others. I made him to enjoy as well as to caretake each other and the earth around him.

My plan to increase his capabilities and his responsibilities is true with you today. You need not shrink from the new challenges before you. I will be true to My word to make provision for your needs.

Look to this beginning as an adventure, an opportunity to express yet another part of yourself.

Get Yourself Conditioned

You are wise to set time aside to come before Me at the beginning of your day. Although I have My plans for you, there are, indeed, other forces besides Mine with ideas for your day that are not in your best interest.

Get yourself conditioned early to spend even a few moments, though longer would be better, to familiarize yourself with what it feels like to be in My presence. As you think of Me ask what I would have you accomplish this day.

Think of those you anticipate seeing, asking what My plan is for your interchange or discourse. Talk to Me of your hopes and desires for the day and hold before Me your questions and fears.

Give Me but a moment to guide you with a thought, an idea, a picture. Do not be quick to continue in monologue. I too, have things to share.

If day upon day, year upon year you do not recognize Me as a partaker of the fruits of your life, you fail to understand the importance of this time wisely spent.

Trust me to order your days in all measures of the needs around you. Trust Me to provide for your needs as well that the abundant life of My design is for you insured.

Milk to Wine

You are beginning a new undertaking where your scope of influence reaches further than before. It is My design to use your work to speak confidences to some, and to others, healing.

Stay close. Stay close within My presence for the enemy has other designs than what I plan. He stands to lose great contingents from his army by your bringing My presence into his camp.

Don't worry that this challenge is too great for you. You have matured from milk to the wine of My Holy Spirit, who will carry you through in victory for My name's sake.

Joy of Purpose

There are other things that I have for you not presently in the forefront of your thoughts or even your dreams. You are being readied now as are those whose abilities are to be used for you.

It sometimes seems that your time on earth will expire before any rewards of your labor come to fruitfulness. You imagine that to be the case for many around you whose lives seem barren. Even knowing that it is not fair or just to judge the quality of another's life, you nevertheless express discontent that your life might be lived in such seemingly apparent lack of usefulness.

Know well that My plans unfold with a timing that is precise in their perfection for My use. Be patient in waiting. Lay your hopes and dreams before Me that in perfecting them, I may bring you great joy of purpose.

The Artist's Palette

Here is My message to you concerning the turmoil now crowding My people of different colors. Oh, how I long to infect the world with the wonder of this creative artistry!

Would you take a palette of the finest oils, the richest hues and discard all but the few that bring you the greatest pleasure? Can you paint all shades of light and dark by putting to your brush such a limited range of your medium?

My medium is people. I have a place where each is needed to complete My purpose. My need is to find them available and ready for service, pliable in the Master's hand.

Building Endurance

As you go now to fill those areas of need you suspect are required of you to fill, I understand that your heart goes not with the task. You think your satisfaction comes after all distasteful or monotonous work is done. These things are needed for completion of duties.

Yes, I have redirected your duties to My satisfaction, and yours is to be tried and tested before dawning with joy. I am working in you a perseverance, a stick-to-it-tiveness that builds your endurance to the level of My calling.

All is not joy. All is not ease of accomplishment. You have been so blessed with capabilities that coming face to face with more monumental requirements finds you giving up before their end is in sight. You have forgotten what it means to press toward the goal, to fight the good fight believing increase will come as you ask it of yourself.

I ask you to learn again to hope. Intellectually, you know that to have hope means to have faith in that which is unseen.

Now, I ask you to work for that thing in which you do not see the end. Although you find no great joy, continue with determination which, in itself affords a sense of pride.

Put the learning of this into your bag of talents so that it may be withdrawn at moment's notice. Do it with genuine peace of heart and mind, knowing My hidden purpose will bless you.

Gifts of the Father

From the Father come the rich blessings imparted unto you. There are times you realize this, such as when love for someone in passing overwhelms you. You have recognized that without the Father's passionate love coming down, in, and through you this would not be possible.

It is in this way that the Father blesses some who otherwise would not receive His gifts. Thank you for your willingness to be so used.

How much sooner would My world be healed if more people gave themselves in whole of heart, mind, and body for this work.

Closer Than a Prayer

Now comes quickly the time to draw in around you these who are your loving support. Now is that time to ask for unity of heart and mind concerning your call to action before Me.

They may not understand the urgency with which you go or your willingness to leave your comforts behind to answer My call. But I have consolation for them and lessons to give them in bidding you Godspeed.

My dreams have been long in the making for you. Happenings and contacts of which you deemed little importance were part of My integral plan to get your mind and heart ready for your mission.

Yes, your mission is about ready to unfold before you and My purposes are going to be apparent to you and to many others who will be watching.

Who will be most astonished to see Me work in you to touch the hearts of others? Who will be willing to change their own life-call because of seeing the joy and determination of your work?

Do not be concerned about the course your loved ones' lives may take apart from you. I have them, too, in My hand and will guide their learning into growth experiences unequaled to any they have known.

Go with the message of My great love and compassion. I send you to multiply the harvest of Mine own. With you I am always closer than a prayer.

News of the Fire

Even at this time are My armies preparing against the day of battle. Like nothing the peoples of the earth have seen is that day coming to bring home My Word. Be a part of this army and I will give ministering angels to shield and protect you for My sake and for My kingdom's victory.

Do you hear the rumblings even now? They have begun to echo across your land as well as lands so distant as to try to divide the forces they seek to devour. It is a time of preparation, a time to begin revealing on whose side you war.

Not for much longer will I be a God whose tender mercies and compassion wait on the cries of those lost ones. No, I must go ahead in strength to claim Mine whose names are before Me.

You are to be sent out with a warning to forsake today's idols of greed and perversions, with a plea to seek My forgiveness. My children are being prepared and girded up with news of the fire of My Holy Spirit that this fire may consume them in passion for My work.

Ask of yourself, "What must I do to get ready?"

Desire to Trust

You have seen how I have taken away your fear of horses and replaced it with respect and a robust appreciation shared at your encounters. There are needs among each of My creations which only I understand and for which I also provide.

It pleases Me to watch creatures so different in design enjoying each other. The vulnerability brought to such meetings expresses a desire to establish trust.

Never confuse an aloofness or a social ineptness in someone with personal rejection of you. Consider that their level of trust may not yet prove a worthy proffer.

I ask you to teach a measure of trust by offering it. No bold bearing is needed, only an open mind and listening heart. Acceptance on the first level of recognition is the foundation stone. Become more loving, that judgmental thoughts not be a stumbling stone for the building of trust.

Pray for the Children

This bursting forth of children around you is a part of My plan to fill the world with workers for the kingdom. They are indeed a wiser and gentler nation, but they are to be bold and strong as never before.

Where I send them I have great hope for those under whose care they are placed, whose call as under-shepherds has been spoken.

More than ever it is important that you pray over them for their guidance and their protection. More than ever it is My hope that they respond to the bending and shaping of their lives' direction as I find fit. This will bless as will no other part of their life at My bidding and in My sovereign will.

Pray to become divinely used to prosper My children in their brief sojourn there.

Brotherhood

To you new Christians, stay close in the faith. That is, stay in the presence of godly fellowship. No sooner than you have professed to believe that Jesus Christ is Lord there will be an onslaught of spirits both in the heavens and on earth to come against you and to weaken the very beliefs so newly born in you.

It is in these times when the shoot is so tender that the worms seek to devour it. You who are tender in the joy and knowledge of your faith must be made strong in order to resist and overcome that which has been cleverly disguised by the enemy to cause you to fall.

To you who are strong in the faith I say, take seriously your responsibility to teach these newly born into the kingdom.

Without guidance from more wise and mature Christians, they may lose sight of their first excitement and become so discouraged as to retreat into confusion.

Form early a brotherhood for new Christians, a place of learning and edification. How difficult it is to grow up in the spirit without the companionship of likeminded friends.

Take care to provide a shelter and a rock that their faith be established a firm and mighty stronghold.

Ask to be Taught

Is it discipline you pray to receive? It is true that discipline is spoken of in My word as self-control. This is an important lesson. This does not mean abusing yourself or allowing guilt or discouragement to overtake your efforts.

Remember that it was said to take everything to Me in prayer? Prayer in itself requires a discipline. Begin there, asking the Holy Spirit to lead you in this converse. Ask that you be taught how to war against any stronghold that keeps you captive.

Make Yourself Teachable

Start now as you would any task to which you bring little knowledge but great anticipation of learning. I have chosen ones as mentors among whom you may grow to be introduced as you become available in heart and mind.

Remember that I told you I would both prepare you and the ground on which you were to toil. Your act of faith in My provision first takes you to one I place in your path for guidance. How I enjoy giving My followers a teachable and eager student.

Here, then, is your immediate task. Make yourself teachable. Keep your mind alert to My working in you through your tutor. Share the joy of accomplishment of even small things with him and with Me.

In all things praise Me and give Me thanks that I love you so much to have planned for every step of your journey. If you will trust Me to fulfill what I have spoken, you will find I am faithful to My word.

Treasures of My Gentleness

Remember now that child of five lying on her back in the field in tall grass beyond her house. Believed to be hidden from view, you blew that yellow plastic bird-shaped whistle as a call to My feathered ones to come to you.

Those were times of communion with Me that I cherished for you were learning of My great love for all My creations. In that time your spirit found joy as I intended all men to find, lying in quiet among the treasures of My gentleness.

Because you have responded to My call to commune with Me in nature I give it back to you now, entrusting it to you to share with others seeking this same solitude. You will bear in mind those same lessons I gave you when you plan and purpose every usable acre.

Look to the mountains and I will pour out My blessings in abundance to all who enter the gates of My abiding there with you. Her pastures will contain a herd of goats, a flock of geese, a meadow for flowers of all seasons. And you will choose workers whose delight it is to help you maintain the land.

Lay Down Self-will

Blessed is he who comes in the name of the Lord, for I give an anointing for peace and revelation, that all who pay heed to his call will come into the kingdom.

There are false prophets already among you following after lies that appear as godly messages. They seem as godly messengers with words of knowledge flowing from another realm.

Did I not say to you that this would take place before the return of the Lord to earth? Did I warn you not to believe everyone who says, "I come in the name of the Lord"? Do these whose wisdom is counterfeit also tell you the end result of belief in them? No.

Who would knowingly choose the eternal anguish his spirit would feel in the absence of peace? In the absence of comfort? Whose only joy is claimed at pain equally shared with those counterparts of the dark world?

Hear how I call My own the sheep of My pastures. Lay down your self-will that determines to find your place in the universe among those who call themselves god. There is more peace and more power than your imagination can hold when you become as one of My sheep, led by Me and fed by My Word.

Lessons of My Love

You are setting out now on a journey of great importance. Don't hesitate or look back for I am here to hold you up during every maneuver needed to overcome the depths and the wilds as they come against you.

You will see My blessings overtake you even as you traverse the hard places. I could be more specific, but you would not even trust the specifics.

I could reveal the downfalls and your uprisings, but you must experience them for maximum growth. I have so much planned for your growth and for your usefulness in My kingdom that you could not even anticipate how it would happen.

Consider My lessons as lessons of My love for you. Consider that I am bringing you through storms in order to plant your feet high and dry on ground where nothing can hurt your progress or tear your path from under you.

I am opening even this moment the mouths of these coming to take their pleasure in your success. You will know them as worshippers of the true God.

Beyond These Words

Your book, even this very book that is of My design and My words to you, this book is nearing the final chapter.

I understand your desire to continue in communication with Me. I know you have delighted in meeting daily with Me to receive these gifts.

I am not leaving you. Rather, I am taking you beyond these simple words to other means of working My work with Me. The joy has only begun!

My World Awaits

A final word is to be given. My world awaits the coming of a new age wherein new hope will offer peace from nation to nation, and true compassion between her peoples.

Now, strife follows strife. Tears of the spirit continue to flood barren, weary souls, and all the while each one hopes for answers: "How long before our peace?" "Is this but the ending, or are we entering a time of beginning on another realm?"

Hear the distant rumblings and recognize them as warnings of false proclamations. Do not quickly follow after one who seems to offer peace for nations, yet whose heart's true desire is hidden from view.

Deception has filled that which appears to overflow with many good things. In the days when man appears as the divine, you must know that I have not yet appeared. This too, must happen for the fulfillment of prophecy.

Send forth the pages written here to places I have prepared to receive them. How I want to bless you! How much greater is My desire to bless My wandering lambs!

Look to the seas and remember how I divided them to make a way for My people. I will open them for you that you may go and share the hope of My coming and the promise of the abundant life found in My presence.

My truth will reign. I have spoken.